THE ANTIDOTE TO GREED

The Healing Power of Habitual Giving

NICK KEOMAHAVONG

MICHAEL VIRADHAMMO

ILLUSTRATOR AND COVER DESIGNER
Venerable Tim Dhiranando

In Loving Memory of
John George Kokoska

1958 - 2023

This book is dedicated to Venerable Michael's father, John, who passed away a mere two months before this book's release date. May the giving spirit that John embodied live on through this book, and may he fully receive all the goodness and merit that the guidance of this book generates in the life of you, the reader, and in the lives of those around you.

TABLE OF CONTENTS

PREFACE

This book is a practical guide that will help you progressively eliminate greed—one of the deepest sources of human suffering—from your mind while simultaneously helping you cultivate genuine contentment through the practice of generosity. Although generosity is by no means a virtue unique to Buddhism and stands as a topic that we likely have all learned about in some capacity, many people still struggle with doubts and a lack of clarity about how to perform acts of giving effectively and in a way that fits for their specific set of circumstances. And so, this book was created to address such issues and present a new approach to this familiar topic.

My goal in writing this book is to unveil the true healing power of habitual giving and provide you with clear guidance on how to incorporate a sustainable habit into your daily life. This guide draws inspiration from select teachings of the Buddha, the wisdom I've learned from the monastery and my teaching monks, and tips and tricks from my own journey of generosity training, combining them into a framework that will help you unlock a more deeply transformative way to give. But don't worry—while these notions do come from Buddhism, the information will be presented and structured in a way that is relatable and applicable to people of *all* belief systems.

On that note, I would first like to clarify that this book is *not* an academic deep dive into all of the Buddha's teachings on giving. There are certain Buddhist teachings on the topic of giving—e.g., ones that require a faith in Karmic laws, rebirth, or the afterlife—that are covered extensively in the scriptures but will *not* be touched upon in this book. My aim here is to focus fully on practicality, not philosophical or religious education. Thus, this book will only elaborate on the universal, nonreligious nature of giving that can help you experience tangible benefits here and now in this lifetime.

This book seeks to help answer the following questions:
- How can I give if I have very little resources?
- Does the amount of the gift truly matter that much?
- Is it selfish to give because it benefits me in some way? If so, how do I give unselfishly?
- How do I give in a way that generates the most benefit for both the giver and receiver?
- How often should I give, and to whom?
- What types of giving are there?
- How can giving help me meditate better?
- How can giving help me sleep better?
- How can giving help me pass away in a more peaceful state?
- How do I find a balance between taking care of my own needs and giving to others?
- Is forgiveness a type of giving? If so, how can I forgive those who have hurt me?

The theory section will provide you with simple and straightforward analogies, stories, and explanations to help you understand why a habit of giving is worth the effort it takes to establish. Afterwards, the practical stepwork will guide you through the process of both identifying a way of giving that deeply resonates with you and crafting a plan of action to fit this practice of generosity into your daily schedule in the most seamless way possible.

Before we dive in, I want to congratulate you on picking up this book and acting on the intention of incorporating positive change into your life. It is truly an act of courage to look inwards, expose the darkness within the mind, and strive to overcome it, thus cultivating a more wholesome version of yourself. This is the journey you are about to undertake. I commend your intention, and I am excited to support you every step of the way on this road to inner transformation. So, without further ado, let's get started!

INTRODUCTION

A Turning Point

I'd like to tell you about the darkest period of my life. (I know—that escalated quickly!) And I'm sorry to go from 0 to 100 in one sentence, but I know that so many people nowadays are entrenched in a depth of suffering and in desperate need of hope. Hope that there are simple, practical steps you can take toward genuine healing. Hope that things can and *will* get better with the right approach. And so, it is my hope that this little window into how I slowly but steadily came out of my dark night of the soul might provide a little bit of just that.

Let's start by rewinding a decade or so, back when I was in my late twenties. Life was great. I had a brand-new four-bedroom house in San Marcos, California, a beautiful girlfriend of five years, a booming real estate career, and a spot on a professional hip-hop dance team that was touring around the world. As an immigrant who had spent the first five years of my life in refugee camps, I felt like Leonardo DiCaprio on the front of the Titanic. I was king of the world! The decades of hard work had paid off, and the American dream was mine.

But my picture-perfect life was exposed to be as transient as a dream when I received the dreaded message from my girlfriend: "We need to talk." The tone of that one statement said it all. This was the beginning of the end for me—the end of a relationship that I had thought would last a lifetime. The end of my certainty that I knew who I was, what my values were, and what I was supposed to do with my life. The end of my American dream . . . and the beginning of my nightmare.

To hear that the woman I loved didn't have those same feelings for me anymore absolutely destroyed me. It sent me into a deep downward spiral. I felt betrayed, lost, and utterly alone. As I walked up the staircase of my now-empty four-bedroom house, I wondered what it was I had worked so hard for. What was the purpose of having such nice things if you had nobody to share them with? Life lost its luster, and for the next few months, I hardly had the will to get out of bed.

At my darkest, I sought out my mother for advice. I went to her, broken heart in hand, and tearfully asked why this was happening to me. How could I move on and heal from a wound that had cut me to the quick and shook me to the very core of my being?

As a devout Buddhist, my mother very matter-of-factly told me, "Nick, right now, you are simply paying off your Karmic debts. The only way to move forward is to avoid making any more bad Karma, and focus on doing as much good as possible."

I have to admit . . . in that moment, I did not feel very consoled by this sentiment. I think I was really in search of emotional support and coping mechanisms to lessen the heaviness on my heart—and I certainly found those things once I began doing one-on-one sessions with a life coach. But as I started to stabilize, I was drawn back to the wisdom that my mother had shared with me, and I started to apply her advice.

With her words in mind, I started seeking out opportunities to give. Whether that was small donations to the temple, helping others in need, or any other random acts of kindness, I made it a point to not allow a single day go by where I did not give. I slowly incorporated giving into a daily practice that became integrated into the fabric of who I was as a person. Instead of just taking from the world by amassing material possessions, collecting accolades, and other-wise checking off the tick boxes on Western society's definition of success, I began to balance what I hoped to receive with at least an equal amount that I gave back.

And, in doing so, I shifted my paradigm—from someone who only seeks to take to someone who genuinely seeks to give. And each act of generosity, bit by bit, served to reduce the heaviness that clouded my world.

How to Stop Being So Salty

In the following chapters, I go into more detail about the steps I took on my personal path of cultivating a generosity-based paradigm and intermix lessons from the Buddhist wisdom I've learned from the monastery. This blend of personal anecdotes, Buddhist concepts, and practical stepwork will help answer all of the questions found in the preface and provide guidance on how to apply what you've learned.

This book, of course, focuses on giving specifically, but when giving is combined with two other wholesome habits, it creates a universal three-pillar model to help anyone overcome their suffering and cultivate genuine inner peace, compassion, and wisdom. So, to paint the bigger picture of this self-transformation model, let's take a quick look at these pillars now.

The three habits include morality, meditation, and finally, giving. Or, if you want to break these practices down into simple, action-based descriptions, we could label them as the daily commitments to: stop doing bad, purify the mind, and do more good. In Buddhism, these are called *the three bases of meritorious deeds* that help the practitioner create more brightness of mind while avoiding the creation of any more darkness of mind.

This trio of wholesome habits empowered me to lift myself out of a depth of suffering and orient my life in a more meaningful, fulfilling direction. To understand how these practices can help us move on from a difficult stage in life and continuously push us in a positive direction, let's make an analogy.

Let's imagine—like we do so often with Buddhist analogies—that your mind is like a glass of water. The eight ounces of pure, crystal clear water contained within this glass represents all the wholesome things you have ever done. On the other hand, the hefty, heaping scoop of salt that you're about to add to that water represents all of the times where you harmed yourself or others through the way you thought, spoke, or acted. Now, imagine that you stirred in all the salt and took a big gulp of that water. How would it taste? Pretty salty, right?

So, how do we reduce the salty taste of this water? Can we just reach in and pull out all of the salt particles? Not really. Once the salt has been dissolved, this technique is simply not possible. So what do we do instead? Well, firstly, it's important not to add any more salt! That would be counterproductive. Secondly, all we need to do is just add more pure, clean water to dilute the salt. Imagine you filled your glass up to the top and then took that glass and poured it into a five-gallon drum. Next, imagine you continue adding more pure water while refraining from adding any more salt. Now, once the drum is full, you pour it into a big bathtub. Once the tub is full, you transfer the solution over to a big empty swimming pool and continue to fill it up until it is brimming with water.

Although I generally don't recommend drinking pool water, let's imagine—for the sake of the analogy—that you stuck your face into the pool and took a big gulp of the water. How would it taste now? Assuming that nothing else besides clean water had been added since the beginning of this process, that water would no longer taste salty in the slightest. Did the salt magically disappear? Nope—there is still the same amount of salt in the water now as there was when you took that first extremely salty sip. The difference is, the salt has been progressively diluted by adding more pure water.

From a Buddhist standpoint, this is the same way in which we overcome our suffering. Firstly, we stop "adding salt," or engaging in speech and behavior that causes harm to ourselves and others. We covered this first practice in depth in *The Buddhist Cleanse*, but as a quick recap, the five precepts (or "protective shields") are to refrain from: destroying living creatures, taking that which is not given, sexual misconduct, false speech, and consumption of intoxicants. Secondly, the way to add more "pure water" in order to dilute the salt is to practice meditation and generosity. And again, this book will be focusing specifically on how a habit of generosity affects the mind, so that is what we will elaborate on now.

Every time that we give, bright and pure energy is generated within the mind. And I won't just ask you to accept this on faith alone—you can actually feel this process in action. I want to invite you now to reflect and bring to mind the most impactful instance you can remember where you did a random act of kindness, engaged in some form of community service, or provided aid to someone in need in any capacity. Reconnect with how you felt in that moment. Perhaps there was a warm glowing sensation in your chest or somewhere else in your body. Maybe it was so powerful that it brought you to tears in that moment, or perhaps it has that same emotional effect even now as you reminisce and reconnect with that memory.

That feeling—one that is so visceral, it is accompanied by a noticeable somatic effect—indicates the presence of something within your mind that has the power to heal your suffering. Something that has the power to uproot a self-serving paradigm and establish a generosity-based one. Something that can deeply shift and transform your entire life in a more positive direction. In Buddhism, this is called "merit" or "puñña," but to make this term a bit more universal, we can just call it brightness of mind or positive spiritual energy.

Any time that you meditate or perform an act of generosity, this positive spiritual energy arises within the mind. The more effectively you are able to still the mind in meditation and the more purely you are able to give, the brighter the mind becomes. Although this energy is not of the physical world, anyone who has had a memorable meditation experience or performed an impactful act of generosity knows from experience that you can viscerally *feel* the presence of that spiritual energy within the body and mind.

When you are able to generate this brightness of mind through a habit of intentional giving, it serves to progressively dilute and displace the heaviness that may currently occupy your mind. Oftentimes, our minds can be burdened by remorse or guilt of past transgressions where we harmed others or ourselves. Or traumatic events from our past can replay in our minds over and over again, entrenching us in a negative headspace. Perhaps we tend to suffer from a generally pessimistic and overly critical outlook on life.

These types of mental patterns can serve to keep us in a rut. But when we learn how to interrupt those patterns by generating brightness of mind and cultivating the ability to carry that feeling with us, we don't need to rely so heavily on three daily quad espresso shots or a tirade of inspirational quotes to keep us positive and motivated. Rather, positivity and motivation will arise naturally from within us after undergoing the generosity training outlined in this book. As you apply these principles to dilute the heaviness of the past with the brightness of generosity, your entire world will shift. And in the process, you will certainly become a less salty individual . . . even if you already happen to be pretty sweet by nature. :)

Purify Your Paradigm: The Antidote to Greed

Now that we have a good idea of how giving—practiced alongside our other two wholesome habits—can help us cultivate a happier, lighter state of being, let's take it one step further. What are the specific ways that intentional, habitual giving shifts us? How does it reach into the fabric of our paradigm and transform the entire way in which we view ourselves, others, and the world around us?

To explain this, let's define the purpose of giving in the context of this book. People give for many different reasons. Sometimes we give because it makes us feel all warm and fuzzy inside (and you now, of course, have a deeper understanding of what that warm fuzziness is). Sometimes the praise, esteem, status, and reputation that we receive as a result of giving is what fuels us. Maybe we give to earn a favor from someone, or to return one. Maybe we give out of obligation, because we've been taught since childhood that giving is what we're "supposed to do" in order to be a good person.

The purpose of giving, the role that it plays, and the need it fulfills in each person's life definitely varies depending on that person's specific perspective. But in this book, we will break down the practice of giving primarily as "a way of training the mind." The Buddha recognized that giving was one of the most accessible forms of purifying the mind for beginners, because most people already have direct experience with this practice in their daily lives. Therefore, this was typically the first thing he taught to individuals who had little to no conceptual foundation or experience in spiritual development. He helped such students understand the deeper purpose of giving, how it affects the mind, and how to give in the most purifying way.

So, since this book elaborates on giving as a way of training the mind, we can define giving as an act by which we let go of something valuable that belongs to us and provide it to someone else for the purpose of releasing greed and cultivating brightness within the mind.

Before we move on, it's important to also provide a definition for greed in this context. Often, when we think of the word "greed," public figures who blatantly embody this trait quickly come to mind. Corrupt, powerful individuals who exploit others for personal gain on a large scale are easy targets, and yes, they do play a large part in some of the most egregious global issues that we face. But it's also important to understand that the force driving such immoral behavior exists in all of us, and it affects the way that all unenlightened beings think, speak, and behave to a certain extent.

Simply put, greed is a self-centered desire for more. From wanting more food, money, power, influence, fame, material possessions, pleasure, status, excitement, achievements, praise, recognition, friends, love, affection, attention, and so on and so forth, greed shows up in various ways in a wide variety of contexts, and it affects us all to varying degrees. The mind is stirred up into a state of greed when we experience or think about something we like and crave— wishing for this experience to persist or to increase in magnitude.

Under the grips of greed, we can experience jealousy, lust, or other such mental states where we are attached to whatever it is we want to have, become, or prolong and maintain. This mental impurity frames the world in a way in which we view the people and situations around us as a means to get our needs met. Greed often causes us to disregard the negative side effects that our behavior has on others or, ultimately, even ourselves. In the end, our own insatiable craving trumps all empathy and long-term thinking.

As a result of greed-driven mental states, we begin to interact with the world in a selfish, transactional way. We plan. We plot. We pray. We manifest. Our thoughts, speech, and behavior reflect our intentions to manipulate the world into delivering us that which we cannot get enough of. But even when the craving is gratified or the goal achieved, the satisfaction is short-lived. We can overlook what we already have by constantly comparing ourselves to others who have something that we desire to a greater degree than we do. We then fall prey to feelings of lack and inadequacy. Contentment eludes us. We get locked into a perpetual pursuit of happiness.

This is the pernicious nature of greed, and elaborating on how it affects our lives in this way can help us to appreciate just how important it is for us to take measures to uproot it and counteract the influence it has on our minds and lives. The bit of bad news is: When we are not mindful, it is very easy for greed to strongly influence how we think, speak, and behave. Our consumerist world, with its finite resources, abundance of competition, and limitless needs and wants, is a fertile ground for greed to grow. In fact, behaving in a slightly or even overtly greedy fashion is justified by basic economics; we are deeply conditioned to believe that it is the most surefire way to survive and be successful in life. Hustle.

Grind. Save. Build. Collect and protect your resources. Give only when there is an opportunity to gain. This mental impurity can easily infect our paradigm and deeply define the way we view and interact with the world.

But now for the good news: With a shift in perspective and the incorporation of a few simple daily steps, you can displace this internal disposition to just *take* from the world and replace it with a genuine disposition to *give*. We can define this internal disposition to give as generosity. And when you take the time to cultivate a generosity-based paradigm, it will deeply transform your outlook on life and how you show up in the world. You and those around you will benefit greatly as a result.

This book serves as an invitation to reposition some of the excessive energy and focus many of us spend searching for happiness in the outside world to peer, instead, into our own inner world. By bringing our eyes back from achieving, attaining, and doing more while constantly comparing ourselves to others, we can start to shed light on the areas where greed manifests in our own lives. This refocusing of attention is not for the sake of exposing "how bad of a person you are," but rather to identify one of the main root causes of our suffering. When you can do the courageous work of illuminating your own shadow side—or your blind spots where you fall short of the ideal version of yourself—you empower yourself to overcome that darkness. And as one of the deepest root causes of your suffering starts to dissipate, a more sustainable form of happiness naturally arises.

By training the mind with intentional and habitual giving, we can uproot the force that actively keeps us from never truly understanding the word "enough." When we release the grips of greed on the mind, we start to truly feel that we *have* enough, *are* enough, and *have done* enough in this moment. We can experience true contentment here and now. Now, this doesn't mean that we stop progressing or striving for a better situation, materially and otherwise, for ourselves and those around us—not at all. Rather, we continue to develop our lives in whichever ways we like, but we do so with a new deep, genuine gratitude for where we are in this moment. Bit by bit, our entire paradigm of how to live a happy, fulfilling, and meaningful life will shift. Instead of the greed-based paradigm that a consumerist culture ingrains in our psyche, a generosity-based paradigm and its positive results will arise.

Greed-Based Paradigm	Generosity-Based Paradigm
Seeks to take	Seeks to give
Main source of happiness comes from more resources, status, and praise	Main source of happiness comes from being of service to others
Speaks and behaves with hidden, selfish motives	Speaks and behaves with pure, selfless motives
Jealous of the success of others	Rejoices in the success of others
Dissatisfied	Content
Relationships are transactional	Relationships are based on genuine connection and service
Competitive	Cooperative

Win-lose mentality	Win-win mentality
Always too busy to help others	Makes time to help others
Attached to belongings and stresses over their acquisition and protection	Generous with their belongings and does not despair if they are separated from them
Gives only to earn a favor or get something in return	Gives because the act itself brings the giver joy
Holds on to resentment and does not forgive	Works toward forgiveness and letting go of toxic emotions toward those who have wronged them

Of course, this list is not necessarily exhaustive, and it's also not so black-and-white. Everything exists on a spectrum; perhaps there are specific contexts and situations where we operate more from a generosity-based paradigm and others where greed takes the reins. But empowered with this lens and the table above, you will be able to more clearly see the various characteristics of each paradigm, which will then clue you in to which attributes to work toward releasing and which to cultivate. Now, you have a framework to more easily observe yourself and accurately identify areas in your life where you can improve.

And maybe, as you read this list with a genuinely open and self-reflective state of mind, you noticed that some of the descriptions from the greed-based paradigm ring true for you. Maybe you'll even notice them popping up in your daily life moving forward. It is perfectly normal and natural for this realization to be a bit uncomfortable, disheartening, or painful, and if it did feel this way for you, I just want to say: "Welcome. And well done." Most people don't take the time or effort to clearly see such parts of themselves precisely because of this pain or discomfort, but I want to assure you that *this* is where genuine spiritual progress and transformation happens.

Embracing these uncomfortable aspects of our shadow side with a neutral state of observation allows us to eventually overcome them. Seeing yourself clearly and with neutrality is the first step. So, try to be kind and soft and refrain from judging yourself too harshly. The clarity you gain as you observe yourself with this new lens and apply the stepwork provided in this book will help you shift your life deeply. It will kickstart the process of progressively embodying each of the positive qualities from the generosity-based paradigm. Just remember to maintain this kindness to yourself as you start this journey of looking within. This gentle approach will help you more effectively discover one of the deepest root causes of your suffering and take steps toward eliminating it at the source.

And to be clear, I make no assumptions about where you are at this moment! Perhaps you are very well-balanced and healthy at this point in your life, and if that's the case, I hope this book empowers you to sustain that state into the future and increases your capacity to spread your reserves of positivity to many people around you.

But on the other hand, it's also possible that you're in a space of darkness similar to where I was during my breakup. Perhaps your situation is much more dire than mine was. Regardless of the details, I want to reassure you that you c*an and will* turn things around. It won't be easy. It won't be glamorous. But speaking from experience, it *will be worth it.* There will be a point down the road when you wake up, take a deep breath, and recognize, "Wow, life feels less heavy. I finally feel like I can breathe again." And at that point, you will be able to look in the mirror and genuinely say, "I feel proud of myself. I worked hard to overcome that darkness inside, and I have earned this brightness of mind that I currently feel."

This book stands as a companion for your journey containing everything I wish I'd had as I was seeking to "dilute the salt" of my past and create a better life for myself. I am excited for you to experience the many positive benefits in store for you on this path that now—with this book in hand—you are very well equipped to travel. With that, it is now time for you to start consuming the antidote to greed and discovering the true healing power of habitual giving. Without any further ado, let's get to work!

CHAPTER I
THE FIVE TYPES OF GIVING

Giving as a form of mind training is a process that involves releasing something that is both valuable to us and can be of benefit to others. Whether that is money, food, resources, time, energy, advice, wisdom, or even forgiveness, there are many different types of giving that can be effective at relinquishing greed and attachment to our physical and nonphysical belongings. As a result of this generosity training, the mind becomes more pure, free, and bright.

This chapter will provide you with definitions for five overarching categories of giving followed by a list of subcategories to further clarify what each type of giving entails, split up into acts done to organizations as well as individuals. While these lists may not include every single possibility out there, they will serve as a good starting place for you to consider the options available to you. They may even spark your own ideas of how to give to individuals in your life or inspire further research to identify a charitable organization focused on a cause you resonate with once you start creating an implementation strategy at the end of the book. The types of giving that we will look at are as follows:

- Gifts or donations of money
- Donating, gifting, or sharing physical items
- Volunteering your time, labor, energy, and skills
- Sharing wisdom
- Giving forgiveness

Gifts or Donations of Money

Monetary gifts or donations are perhaps the simplest, most accessible, and most common form of giving. This category can be more specifically defined as providing an individual, a group of people, or an organization with a monetary gift or donation independent or in excess of paying for the cost of a good or service. This could be in the form of cash, a check, an electronic transfer, cryptocurrency, or—as a less liquid and readily usable option—stocks. Since money is a medium of exchange that allows the owner to purchase valuable goods or services or pay back debts, it is a gift that has inherent value to everyone and can help directly support the incredible diversity of needs and wants from person to person. This essentially universal value of money is why it is such a simple and accessible way to practice generosity and support others.

So, let's make the inherent simplicity of monetary gifts or donations even more accessible by listing some specific examples you can try practicing:

To Organizations:

- Charity Donations: Giving money to nonprofit organizations to support their charitable initiatives, including but not limited to humanitarian initiatives addressing poverty, environmental conservation, human rights, disaster relief, animal welfare, and so on.
- Arts and Culture Organizations: Contributing to arts institutions, museums, theaters, and cultural events.
- Healthcare Organizations: Donating to hospitals, clinics, and medical research organizations.
- Educational Institutions: Supporting grade schools, trade schools, and universities to enhance educational opportunities.
- Religious/Spiritual Institutions: Supporting maintenance costs, building projects, or initiatives of your local temple, church, mosque, meditation center, or place of worship.
- Community Development: Contributing to programs that empower communities through infrastructure, education, and economic initiatives.
- Microfinance Institutions: Donating to organizations that offer small loans and financial services to entrepreneurs in underserved areas.
- Youth Organizations: Supporting programs that engage and empower young people through education, leadership, and skill building.
- Disability Support: Donating to organizations that assist individuals with disabilities and promote inclusion.
- Crisis Hotlines: Supporting helplines and organizations that provide assistance to individuals in emotional distress.
- Veterans' Associations: Giving to organizations that provide support and services to military veterans.

- Cancer or Disease Research: Donating to cancer research institutes (or another disease of interest) and organizations dedicated to finding a cure.
- Technology Initiatives: Supporting organizations that provide access to technology and digital skills in underserved communities.

To Individuals:

- Cash Donations: Making a direct monetary contribution to an individual's financial needs or a specific cause.
- Scholarships: Providing funds to support an individual's tuition or costs of school supplies.
- Emergency Relief Funds: Offering financial assistance during crises, such as natural disasters or medical emergencies.
- Religious/Spiritual Figure Support: Making monetary donations to monks, priests, missionaries, rabbis, imams, nuns, or any other religious/monastic individual to support their path of renunciation/devotion.
- Microfinance Loans: Providing a small loan to help an individual start a business or improve their livelihood.
- Family Support: Contributing to a family's financial needs, especially during difficult times.
- Medical Expenses: Assisting with medical bills, treatment costs, or surgeries for an individual in need.
- Funeral Expenses: Donating funds to cover funeral and burial expenses for a deceased person's family.
- Adoption Funds: Contributing to the costs associated with adopting a child.
- Elderly Care: Supporting the elderly with financial assistance for caregiving services or nursing homes.

- <u>Skills Training</u>: Funding vocational or skill development programs for individuals seeking employment.

Donating, Sharing, or Gifting Physical Items

This second category of giving includes either making an official donation to an organization or simply sharing or giving a physical belonging of yours to an individual. Examples of such items are food, clothing, medicine, medical supplies, toys, household items, machinery, tools, raw materials for a building project, electronics, books, and many other things that will be expanded upon below. The great thing about donating physical items, in addition to the cleansing effect it has on the mind, is the fact that it gives you the opportunity to declutter your environment. This can be a very helpful activity when you feel energetically stuck or stagnant, as freeing up space in your surroundings can be an extremely effective way to also free up space within your mind and facilitate the process of coming back into balance.

Before we get into the list of examples, let's discuss a few disclaimers about the appropriateness of physical gifts. It is important to note here that if the item that you are sharing is not new, then it should at least still be appropriately functional (or fresh and delicious, in the case of food) so that the recipient can still benefit from the item. Another factor to consider when donating a physical item is the appropriateness of the gift given the context. Organizations tend to have clear policies about what types of donations they will accept; however, when you plan to share or give a gift to an individual, be sensitive as to whether or not this gift is needed by the recipient. Although surprises can be nice, when there is a doubt about the appropriateness of a gift, it's a good idea to either give the gift in private, use a gift receipt in the event of a new item, or ask the individual beforehand if such a gift would be appropriate and useful to them. This way, you can avoid unintentionally offending someone in a public manner with a gift that they might perceive as inappropriate or suggestive of something embarrassing.

And last, but not least, the gift should not be harmful to the recipient in any way. A gift is not considered "pure" or beneficial to the mind of either the receiver or giver if it promotes or can be used for breaking the five precepts or "protective shields": killing, stealing, sexual misconduct, false speech, and consumption of intoxicants. Examples of such harmful gifts are intoxicants that cloud the mind (such as drugs and alcohol) or weapons, poisons, or traps that will be used to kill other beings.

With these little disclaimers in place, let's get into some ideas of appropriate physical items you can donate or share.

To Organizations:

- Clothing: Donating clothing to nonprofits, such as thrift stores and donation centers, that accept donations of new or used clothes.
- Essentials for Monastics: Providing Buddhist monks or other renunciates or religious figures with basic needs, such as food, clothing, shelter, or medicine.
- Technology: Giving computers, tablets, or other electronic devices to schools, libraries, or nonprofits.
- Vehicles: Donating cars, trucks, or other vehicles to organizations that can use them for their programs.
- Books and Educational Materials: Contributing books, textbooks, and educational resources to schools and libraries.
- Medical Equipment: Providing medical instruments and equipment to healthcare facilities or charitable clinics.
- Toys and Games: Donating toys, games, and recreational equipment to children's shelters or community centers.
- Art Supplies: Giving art materials to schools, art programs, or community centers.
- Personal Care Products: Donating toiletries and hygiene products to shelters and organizations assisting vulnerable populations.
- Furniture: Contributing furniture to homeless shelters, transitional housing, or disaster relief efforts.
- Sports Equipment: Donating sports gear and equipment to youth sports programs or schools.
- School Supplies: Providing pens, notebooks, backpacks, and other school essentials to students in need.
- Cookware and Kitchen Supplies: Donating pots, pans, utensils, and kitchen appliances to community kitchens and food

programs.

- Baby Supplies: Providing diapers, formula, baby clothing, and other baby essentials to parents in need.
- Construction Materials: Donating building materials, tools, and equipment for infrastructure projects in underserved areas.

To Individuals:

- Clothing: Sharing new or gently used clothing, shoes, and accessories.
- Food: Sharing home-cooked meals, baked goods, or produce.
- Toys: Sharing or gifting toys, games, and stuffed animals.
- Books: Lending or gifting books to people who share similar interests.
- Art Supplies: Sharing or gifting art materials like paints, brushes, and sketchbooks.
- Electronics and Gadgets: Gifting or sharing gadgets, chargers, or electronics.
- Music: Creating and sharing playlists, music recommendations, or vinyl.
- Tools: Lending/gifting needed tools and equipment for DIY projects.
- Garden Produce: Sharing fruits, vegetables, or herbs from your garden.
- DIY Arts & Crafts: Giving a gift of something you created yourself, like a knitted scarf, a drawing, a painting, a poem, or something else creative.
- Pet Supplies: Giving pet treats, accessories, toys, or food to friends or neighbors who have pets.
- Fitness Equipment: Lending exercise equipment, yoga mats, or weights to friends looking to stay active.

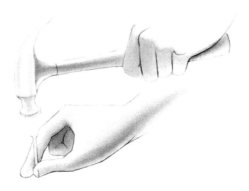

Volunteering Your Time, Labor, Energy, and Skills

This category involves volunteering your time, labor, advice, or expertise to help others. Even though we are not letting go of a physical object that has monetary value, our time and energy are very precious resources that can be of great benefit when offered to others. So, being generous with our time is still certainly an act of giving that relinquishes greed and self-centeredness from the mind.

An additional factor that makes acts of volunteering time and energy uniquely appealing is the increased time commitment. Sometimes, gifts and donations can be made via a very quick interaction that doesn't allow much time for the act to sink into the mind and warm the heart with as much depth as an extended act of service. When you are volunteering your time to help others, on the other hand, you have more face time with the person you're helping, which fosters a closer bond between giver and receiver. This extended exposure can serve to facilitate a more impactful "brightening" of the mind, especially when you train yourself to effectively remain joyful before, during, and after the act—a skill we'll cover in a future chapter.

There are a wide variety of contexts in which we can volunteer our time and energy to others, whether that's by getting involved with organizations centered around community service projects of both short- and long-term natures, going on mission trips to other countries, or even something as simple as helping out a friend or family member who could use a hand.

The list below will elaborate on some of the options available to you and give you a good starting place as you seek to identify a way of volunteering your time that fits for you.

To Organizations:

- Community Cleanups: Participate in organized clean-up events to improve local parks, streets, or natural areas.
- Soup Kitchens: Serve meals at shelters or soup kitchens to help provide food for those in need.
- Tutoring/Mentoring: Offer your expertise via organizations that tutor and mentor students seeking guidance in specific subjects.
- Home Building/Repairs: Help build or repair homes for families in need through organizations such as Habitat for Humanity.
- Hospital Volunteering: Assist patients and staff at hospitals by providing companionship, running errands, or helping with administrative tasks.
- Environmental Conservation: Join conservation groups to

participate in tree planting, habitat restoration, or wildlife protection efforts.

- **Disaster Relief**: Volunteer with organizations like the Red Cross to provide aid during natural disasters or emergencies.
- **Animal Shelters**: Support animal shelters by walking dogs, cleaning cages, and providing care for animals awaiting adoption.
- **Elderly Care**: Spend time with elderly individuals in nursing homes, offering companionship and assistance with daily tasks.
- **Youth Programs**: Engage with children and teenagers through programs like after-school clubs, sports coaching, or arts workshops.
- **Free Technical Consultations/Labor**: If you are a professional or have expertise in a specialized or technical field—such as programming, medicine, architecture, engineering, graphic design, etc.—you can volunteer your expertise via free labor or consultations to charitable organizations in need of your skill set.
- **Mission Trips**: Going on a purposeful journey often organized by a religious or humanitarian group where volunteers travel to a specific location, local or abroad, to provide assistance and support to a community in need.

To Individuals:

- **Moving Assistance**: Help friends or family when they're moving houses by packing, lifting, and unpacking.
- **Childcare**: Offer to babysit for friends or family to give parents a break or help during busy times.
- **Meal Sharing**: Cook meals for friends or family members who may be sick, busy, or going through a tough time.

- Language Exchange: Help someone learn a new language by conversing with them in your native language and learning from them in return.

- Tech Support: Aid friends or family members with tech-related issues, such as setting up devices or troubleshooting problems.

- Completing Someone's Chores: Take someone's dishes after meal time and wash them, fold a family member's laundry, or clean up and organize a shared space.

- DIY Projects: Assist friends with home improvement or DIY projects, providing labor and expertise.

- Gardening Help: Help friends or family members with gardening tasks like planting, weeding, and maintaining their outdoor spaces.

- Resume/CV Review: Offer your expertise to review and provide feedback on resumes or CVs for job-seeking friends.

- Fitness Buddy: Partner with someone who's working on their fitness goals to provide encouragement and companionship during workouts.

- Emotional Support: Be there for friends or family members during challenging times by offering emotional support via a listening ear and/or words of encouragement or advice.

- Smiling: Although this is a rather quick and seemingly insignificant form of giving that may not fit so squarely into this category, smiling is still an act of generosity, as it requires sharing your positive energy with others that you come across. Sometimes a genuine smile that radiates loving kindness can be enough to shift someone's day for the better! So, practice smiling as much as you can to give this uplifting gift to all that you meet. :)

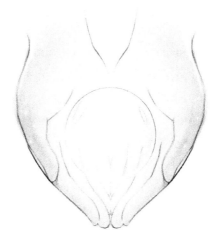

Sharing Wisdom

For our second to last category, we will cover a very special type
of giving: the gift of wisdom. This form of giving is special in the
sense that technically, the items on this list could all fall under other
categories such as providing monetary donations, giving physical
gifts, or providing words of advice. However, the specific subject
matter is what elevates these various forms of giving into its own
category. This type of giving is inspired by the Buddhist concept
of giving the "gift of Dhamma," which refers directly to sharing the
teachings of the Buddha. But for the purposes of universal applica-
bility, we will broaden the scope of this category to include wisdom
from other sources as well. In order to clarify what characteristics
elevate mere knowledge to the level of wisdom, let's elaborate on
what Dhamma is first.

Dhamma has a few translations, but the most simple and common way of explaining this word is as the teachings of the Buddha or the truth of nature. After achieving spiritual enlightenment, the Buddha shared what he discovered by focusing primarily on two things: 1) clearly explaining the deepest root causes of human suffering, and 2) laying out an actionable path that allows practitioners to overcome that suffering at the source. Ultimately, Dhamma clarifies the nature of the human mind and how to train it properly. It guides practitioners to effectively cleanse the impurities of greed, anger, and delusion from the mind, which then allows them to see things clearly, overcome their suffering, and attain a sustainable inner peace and happiness. Unlike other gifts, the gift of Dhamma does not disappear, get used up, or only benefit the recipient for a brief moment. Rather, the new lens of clarity continues to benefit them for the rest of their lives. Due to its deeply beneficial and timeless nature, the Dhamma is considered by Buddhists to be the "highest" gift that creates the most benefit for both the giver and receiver.

With these notable characteristics of the Dhamma properly explained, we can now settle on a definition of "wisdom" that will serve the purposes of this book and clarify the nature of this specific type of giving. We will define wisdom as knowledge that helps you see the conditions of reality clearly and make decisions that create the greatest amount of benefit and decrease the greatest amount of suffering possible for self and others. In essence, wisdom first guides you to see clearly and then guides you to behave skillfully. This definition now provides us with a clearer framework to discern what sources of information, other than the Dhamma, can fit into this type of giving:

- Sacred texts, teachings, or commentaries from any religion or spiritual order
- Mental health knowledge and tools
- Philosophical teachings and practices
- Personal development techniques and resources

As you can see, this category now includes a wide range of material that covers both the entire religious and secular sides of the spectrum. The wisdom that you share with others could be in the form of discussions with friends, family members, or mentees about the knowledge and habits that you have studied and integrated into your life. It could be providing books, videos, audios, or some other form of content to others who are interested in them. Additionally, sharing wisdom could mean providing some form of support—whether monetary or otherwise—to aid some of your favorite sources of wisdom in their dissemination efforts.

The following list contains some of the many different ways to share wisdom with others.

- Run Retreats: Organizing retreats where participants can immerse themselves in intensive study, meditation, teachings, and discussions of wisdom in your desired area of focus.
- Scriptural Study Groups: Form and lead study groups focused on reading, discussing, and applying sacred scriptures and texts.
- Write Books and Articles: Write and publish books, articles, or research papers on the techniques, scriptures, and history of your favorite source of wisdom.
- Make Online Content: Utilize online platforms to make videos, audios, courses, webinars, live-streaming sessions, etc. to

reach a broader audience interested in learning about your wisdom.

- Lend Resources: Lend, gift, or suggest any books or resources that you own or know of to somebody interested in learning more about that type of wisdom.
- Share Quotes: Share inspirational quotes of wisdom on social media platforms.
- Share Personal Reflections: Write blog posts or create vlogs sharing your personal reflections on how various principles of wisdom resonate with your life experiences.
- Listening and Support: Actively listen to others and provide emotional support by sharing teachings that might offer comfort or guidance.
- Artistic Expression: Express your favorite teachings of wisdom through art, music, poetry, storytelling, or other creative outlets.
- Donations: Make a donation to organizations that create books, videos, audios, or other such resources about teachings that you resonate with. In this way, you are actively supporting the gift of wisdom reaching more people.

Forgiveness

Last but not least is another crucial form of giving: forgiveness. Out of all the categories we've covered, forgiveness is the most challenging, and it requires a fair bit of spiritual cultivation and practice over time to perform fully. But despite—or perhaps directly due to—how difficult it is to forgive others or even ask for forgiveness, it stands as an incredibly powerful and transformative way to let go of things we are attached to and cultivate a brighter, happier, more peaceful mind.

Forgiveness is quite a unique form of giving in the sense that it is a very abstract and intangible gift. And although it certainly releases greed from the mind, it is also primarily a profound way of releasing another base impurity from the mind: anger. Forgiveness is the process through which we release feelings of resentment, anger, and ill will toward those who have caused us harm in the past, thus unburdening our hearts.

The wider topic of forgiveness and how to give or ask for it is so deep and significant that it would likely take a full chapter or even an entire book to cover in its entirety. Instead, this section will provide a rather general overview so as not to digress from the focus of this book. From a Buddhist perspective, forgiveness is imperative to reduce or eliminate negative Karmic ties between ourselves and others. Practicing it wholeheartedly will effectively break a repetitive dynamic of suffering between us and them. But perhaps Karma is not a concept that resonates with you so deeply—and that's ok. There are still other, more tangible benefits of forgiveness that can be experienced here and now.

In essence, working toward fully forgiving those who have caused us harm allows us to disempower the past from negatively impacting our present. It doesn't mean that we approve of the person's behavior that hurt us or will allow such situations to happen again, but rather, it means we are working toward releasing the toxicity of resentment, anger, and ill will that continues to cause us suffering in this moment. In situations where we happened to be the one causing harm to another, asking for forgiveness—via giving a sincere, humble apology where we fully own any transgressions without justifying or defending our actions—is another powerful way of reducing heaviness (and negative karmic ties) between ourselves and others.

And the good news is: there are incremental steps you can take on this path that will honor where you are and the degree to which you are capable of giving or asking for forgiveness in this moment. The first way that you can start this practice is at the end of your meditation. Sometimes, we may not be ready to have an interaction with the individual in question, or maybe it will never be appropriate or possible to do so for any number of reasons.

In either case, meditation prepares our mind to be pure, bright, and in a state of greater detachment from heavy emotions. At the end of our meditation, when our mind is peaceful, we simply bring to mind any individuals that we may have harmed in the past—whether we can recall them or not, and whether those beings are living or have passed away—and share this positive energy with them and mentally ask for forgiveness. *Asking* for forgiveness from those who we have harmed is typically an easier process than *sharing* forgiveness with those who have harmed us. This is why it might be more conducive to do the former first. After asking for forgiveness, we proceed to make the intention to mentally forgive any beings who may have caused us harm in the past.

This was a strange process for me as I first started to practice it. Admittedly, it felt a bit fake, like I was lying to myself as I mentally repeated, "I forgive you. May you be happy, healthy, and free from suffering," to the person I still resented. Depending on the depth of the transgression, forgiveness felt all the more contrived and difficult to send to those who had hurt me. But still, I knew I had a deep desire to unburden myself from the heaviness of the past, and so I continued with this practice every day. And with persistence, there was a bizarre moment one day where I spread forgiveness and that familiar constrictive feeling of ill will was no longer present. I *genuinely* wished for that person to be at peace. I could now bring them to mind and feel compassion for how they must have really been suffering to mistreat me so badly. Realizing this, I exhaled with relief and a smile, feeling proud of myself for cultivating a space for forgiveness in my heart. And in cases where someone had made an apology that I previously couldn't accept, it now opened up an opportunity to share with them that I had forgiven them and finally accepted their apology.

This now brings us to forgiveness either shared or asked for in person. The practice of asking for and giving forgiveness in a formal fashion is very common in Thai culture. Before becoming monks, the soon-to-be ordained will bow to their parents and recite the words that include owning up to any past transgressions against or offenses caused to their parents. This ceremony culminates in the child asking for forgiveness and the parents providing it before their child bows once more. The first time I did this, it led to a powerful release of shame and regret and a deep sense of gratitude for my parents' sacrifice to raise me properly. Needless to say, I cried like a baby. It was a very impactful interaction that I am so grateful to have had.

Asking for forgiveness or providing it does not necessarily have to be so ceremonial or formal, but the main takeaway is that doing it in person definitely leads to a more impactful experience, if you are ready for such things. In essence, asking for or giving forgiveness face-to-face is a powerful way to not only reduce or eliminate negative karmic ties, but also to potentially repair damaged relationships. If they don't forgive you despite a humble, genuine apology, your actions will at least provide closure with the knowledge that you did the best you could to make amends.

The following list will provide you with some contexts in which you can ask for or give forgiveness, whether that is in person or after meditation.

People to Ask Forgiveness From or to Forgive:

- Parents
- Siblings
- Children
- Extended family members
- Teachers
- Coaches
- Mentors
- Friends
- Colleagues
- Exes
- Significant others
- Any other beings who we have knowingly harmed (asking forgiveness)
- Any other beings who have harmed us (giving forgiveness)
- Those who have passed away (done after meditation)
- Any other beings we have unknowingly or unintentionally harmed (done after meditation)

CHAPTER II
HOW TO GIVE IN THE MOST HEALING WAY POSSIBLE

Tending to Your Trees Properly

With all of the types of giving thoroughly covered, we have now arrived at the heart of this book. This chapter will provide you with the know-how necessary to train the mind in a way that effectively unlocks the full healing power of giving. The following framework will empower you with the perspective and actionable steps to elevate giving from a mere good deed that momentarily makes you feel good to an act that deeply purifies the mind and shifts your whole life. It will help you maximize both the greed you release and the brightness of mind that you cultivate. This will make the process of giving more enjoyable and, consequently, make the process of creating and sustaining a consistent habit much more effortless.

Oftentimes, when people give without learning this framework, they tend to do so in a very secretive, quick, and nonchalant manner. This style of giving sometimes stems from the fact that these people want to remain humble and not draw any attention to their act of generosity—and, just to be clear, humility and a pure intention to help others without soliciting praise is certainly a good thing that brightens the mind and benefits the recipients! However, giving in this quick, nonchalant way does not allow for the giver to unlock the full purifying potential of that act.

Before we get into the details of how to give in the most healing way possible, let's make an analogy. Let's say you wanted to plant an apple tree in your garden so that you could enjoy its fruit. So, you went out and bought a mature apple tree, quickly dug a random hole in your backyard, and haphazardly planted it. After a bit of time and minimal maintenance, some relatively lackluster apples ripened, you pulled them off of the tree, and you ate them without washing or preparing them in any way. Then, afterwards, you never paid attention to the tree again and left it to die in the backyard.

Now, despite the fact that gardeners across the globe would disapprove of your blasphemous botanical practices, you can't deny the fact that you certainly did succeed in growing and eating some apples. However, there are definitely some areas where improvements could be made to help you maximize your apple yield, increase the deliciousness of the fruit, and extend the life of that apple tree to allow for future harvests.

So, let's reimagine this process in a situation where you grew the apples with more love and care. As you start out, you would take time to make sure you dug the hole in a place with appropriate sunlight for an apple tree. You would then prepare the ground with nutrient-rich soil and fertilizer instead of just packing the normal dirt back into the hole atop the roots. Finally, you would spend a bit more time watering and pruning the tree to make sure it could grow to its full potential.

Then, once it was time for harvest, your hard work would fill your mind with joy as you saw the literal fruits of your labor emerging via apples so beautiful, they'd make Granny Smith jealous! With a wicker basket in hand, you would carefully pluck the ripe fruit and then make your way to the kitchen to wash them thoroughly, slice them up, and enjoy every bite. You might even get fancy and bake some into a pie to share with family and friends.

Then afterwards—having enjoyed the process so much—you would continue to look after that tree with fondness and go on to experience many more fruitful harvests. And each time you saw the tree, it would bring a smile to your face as you felt pride in the work you did to maintain its beauty and enable its healthy growth and bountiful yields. Eventually, this leads you to plant many more trees with similar love and care, and—before you know it—you have an orchard-level amount of apple trees in your backyard. Your passion for this process naturally inspires others to follow in your footsteps and cultivate their own green thumbs as you plant and tend to the trees together. You and all your friends proceed to grow apples, grow old together, and live happily ever after. The end.

Now, how does this analogy relate to the practice of giving? Well, when we give in a relatively nonchalant manner, we still do enjoy some of the fruits of giving. That positive spiritual energy arises, we feel good for a brief moment, and then we go about our day without thinking much about it afterwards. But if we take the time—like the skilled gardener who is attentive and engaged before, during, and after each harvest—to train our mind to be in the proper state before, during, and after each act of generosity, the benefit we derive from each act increases exponentially.

As a result, the brightness of mind generated by each act seeps into the rest of our day as we reflect on the act and enjoy the afterglow. This inspires us to practice more frequently and look for more opportunities to give due to the depth of its uplifting effect. And as we consider these new opportunities to give, our mind further brightens before we even perform the act. We have now unlocked a virtuous cycle that starts to shift our entire paradigm. This provides us with a new, profound source of happiness and positivity that can help us shift our mentality whenever we are in a negative headspace or going through a dark period of life.

Oftentimes, people will tout the benefits of thinking positively and encourage cognitive reframing in order to see the bright side of each situation, and yes, this concept is incredibly important and can be powerful and helpful in some situations. However, at times this can also feel contrived, forced, or like doing mental gymnastics to reframe a negative into a positive. It might even feel dishonest to how we actually feel and serve as a thin veil covering the truth of our inner anguish. Some people might even label this as "toxic positivity," an insistence on focusing exclusively on maintaining a positive attitude which can effectively suppress and minimize the reality of difficult situations.

But instead of merely applying mental effort to *reframe an existing situation*, we can apply physical effort—via an act of giving—to *create a new situation*. In turn, *reframing* simply becomes *refocusing* our attention to a more wholesome object. Good deeds that we perform generate an easily observable positive effect on the lives of others, and such actions create a powerful pattern interrupt that allows us to shift our attention from whatever is weighing heavy on our minds and anchor it to a tangible way in which we've helped others. As we pay attention to the external benefits created by our good deeds, the positive spiritual energy accompanying each act of generosity will naturally grow in tandem. Your generosity training ensures that both your inner world and the world around you become a brighter place.

And as you curate a habit of planting and feeling proud of your *generosi-trees* (Am I overdoing the fruit jokes?), you will amass more and more sources of goodness that not only serve to uplift your mind whenever you feel down, but also naturally raise your base-line mood to be more effortlessly bright, cheerful, and generous. Again, not by reframing, but by refocusing your attention on your habitual practice of good deeds. This powerful habit will serve to progressively uproot the negative qualities of a greed-based para-digm from the mind, firmly plant the qualities of a generosity-based paradigm within, and serve as a shining example that inspires those around us to join in and do the same.

But before we move on, I would like to make a quick disclaimer. It is important to note that following this approach to using acts of generosity to brighten the mind does *not* entail suppressing or avoiding any negative emotions. Please continue to utilize therapy or any other resource that helps you process, understand, and grow through difficult situations in life! This is intended to be a supplement rather than a replacement to your existing healthy forms of self-care.

So, with that being said, let's elaborate on the three distinct phases of giving and how we can train the mind to unlock the full healing power of giving in each phase.

Before the Act of Giving

In the same way that we can prepare the ground and surrounding area to be a fertile, nurturing environment for a strong, healthy apple tree, we can take steps before performing each act of giving to make sure that our mind is primed to receive the full benefits of the act. I would like to use my journey of cultivating a joyful mindset for the before, during, and after phases of giving by sharing the details of the biweekly act of giving that I practiced at the start of my generosity training. Let's focus first on the "before" phase.

I personally found that making a monetary donation to a temple that I visited every two weeks was a great practice for me. The long two-hour drive from San Diego up to the temple in Azusa allowed me to establish a great pre-donation ritual of sorts: I would get up early in the morning, hop in my car, and then obtain the first indispensable ingredient to prepare my mind to be bright and pure . . . a venti iced macchiato from Starbucks. With my caffeinated beverage in hand, I'd roll down the windows and enjoy the beautiful ocean scenery as I merged onto the I-15 headed north for Los Angeles.

I would drink in the fresh morning air and bask in the glow of the morning sun as I played some of my favorite music and enjoyed this peaceful cruise up the coast.

Initially, when I first started making this trip and cultivating this mental space conducive to a fruitful act of giving, there were times when my mind would slip back to my long to-do list and wander to thoughts of doubt. "Is this really worth my time?" "Does giving actually purify the mind in the way the monks shared?" "I could definitely use this money to pay off my upcoming phone bill." "Maybe I could just do a bank transfer instead of wasting half a day making this long trip."

Whenever I noticed such thoughts arising, I recognized that moment as an opportunity to train myself. Those thoughts certainly had logical justifications—I *did* have bills to pay. I *did* also have a social life and my physical health that required time and energy to maintain. Combine these realities with working as a lead clinician supporting twenty therapists at a group home for one hundred foster kids while balancing a professional dance career, my schedule was typically always packed to the brim. But after discovering that all my efforts and achievements in the external world did not truly prepare me with the inner wisdom and resources to handle the darkest time in my life, I recognized that the spiritual dimension of myself was equally as important to spend time cultivating.

I had to prove for myself whether or not the practices that my teaching monks and my mom had shared with me actually worked. And despite the reduced convenience in comparison to an electronic transfer, I wanted to make the donation with my own hands directly to the hands of the recipient in order to feel the act more deeply and train myself to a fuller extent. So, this two-hour drive up to the temple was simply part of my biweekly intensive "spiritual workout" to incrementally uproot the grips of a greed-based paradigm within my mind and establish a generosity-based paradigm in its place.

In each moment that I noticed the self-centered thoughts of regret or doubt arise, I would gently disconnect from them with patience and compassion. I would remind myself that such thought patterns are normal and natural, which would encourage me to not be so hard on myself. Yet, since such thoughts also robbed me of the joy that I might experience from my ceremonial day of giving, I would kindly catch myself in each moment and reconnect with my intention for the trip.

My intention was to transform myself. To transform myself from someone who always just asked from the world into someone who actually gave back. I wanted to release self-centeredness from the mind. To become a genuinely generous person who didn't have ulterior motives backing my actions. I also allowed my mind to fill with gratitude as I reflected on how grateful I was to have a working car, gas, and the monetary resources necessary to give to others. And I felt proud that, despite my busy schedule and a slew of valid excuses, I was sacrificing this time to fight for a better version of me. And I found that making time for this internal battle—that almost nobody knew about—was *absolutely* something to be proud of. So, I trained myself to reconnect and gently rest my awareness in this proud, joyful feeling as consistently as I could, allowing it to cleanse and prepare my mind for a fruitful act of giving.

Now, although the details of other acts of giving could be vastly different from the example I shared above, there are a few crucial takeaways to highlight from this case study. Firstly, if we can create our own fun "pregame" rituals that provide our mind with a bit of extra time to transition into a relaxed, positive mindset, it will make the process of giving both more enjoyable and more cleansing for the mind.

Secondly, if left unattended, it is very easy for the mind to wander to doubt, complaints, and general negativity when preparing for an act of giving. This is normal and natural, and there is no need to be too harsh with ourselves when it happens. The key is to be able to catch ourselves in each of these moments with kindness, patience, and compassion. This allows us to release the natural tendency to feel disappointed due to (inaccurately) viewing these moments as mistakes or indications of how "un-spiritual" we are. Rather, we will start to greet these moments with excitement as we gain an appreciation of them as opportunities to see our patterns clearly and train the mind to detach from them.

And lastly, we can redirect our mind to reconnect with our pure intentions for giving and the positive effects it will have on others and ourselves. We will break down this process into more clear, concise steps in the action plan section toward the end of the book, but for now, let's continue on.

During the Act of Giving

Similar to how we can harvest, clean, and prepare apples from our tree with love and careful attention, thus leading to a more delicious snack, we can also perform an act of giving in a style and state of mind that increases the benefit it generates.

Now let's pick back up where we left off. After the completion of my two-hour drive, I would arrive at the temple and make my way to greet the monks with the envelope containing my donation in hand. The moment I had been mentally preparing for was finally here. And so, with my mind gently resting with all of the positive energy I had collected each morning for two weeks and on the ride up, I made my offering, closed my eyes, and placed my hands in prayer position as I received the sacred blessing from the monk. I was taught that this moment is the most powerful time to make a wish for ourselves and the people we love since the flow of spiritual energy facilitated by this act of giving and sacred chanting is at its peak. So, as the ancient words of Pali emanated from the monk in an entrancing, melodious fashion, I kept my mind still and anchored in this pure, bright, and proud feeling while holding any positive wishes for myself and others gently in mind.

This moment was pure magic. I always felt so present and overjoyed at the completion of this long journey. From the time and effort it took to make the money to the two hour trip of training my mind to be absorbed into a more pure intention, my mission was now complete, and victory was very, very sweet. It may not have been so apparent from the outside looking in—I was just another temple-goer making a routine donation, and the amount was nothing in comparison to many other donors. But for me, I had just won an internal battle and strengthened a spiritual foundation that I knew would serve me for the rest of my life. I knew the importance of this fight, and I allowed myself to be very proud of it as I basked in the afterglow of a job well done.

Now, let's take a moment to extract some essential considerations from this case study to clarify how we can train our mind properly for this "during" phase. Although this phase of giving is relatively brief in the case of making donations, attention and care to keep the mind anchored in that bright positive energy during this phase will still lead to great benefit. This can be a lengthier process in cases where you volunteer your time, so just as we covered in the "before" section, strive to catch yourself kindly when the mind slips to negativity and reconnect with your pure intentions and a positive mindset.

Another key aspect to highlight is the way in which the giving is performed. In the case of donations, being able to give in person— directly to the individual who will receive the gift—is far more impactful than giving electronically or through a donation box. It facilitates the building of a relationship between giver and receiver and allows the receiver to share some gesture of acceptance or appreciation, such as a blessing, words of gratitude, or simply a conversation that strengthens your bond. So, whenever possible, making time for face-to-face donations or acts of service while maintaining a joyful state of mind sets the conditions for the most deeply cleansing, beneficial, and impactful act of giving possible. However, if an electronic donation is the only viable option that you can complete consistently, then that is absolutely ok as well.

After the Act of Giving

Similar to how we can continue to care for an apple tree after harvest so that it can continue to be beautiful and produce more fruit, there are a number of ways we can recollect our good deeds so that they further brighten the mind even after the act is complete.

With my donation to the temple officially made and my blessing received, the time soon came when I needed to make the journey back home. And I must say: at this point, the two-hour drive back to San Diego felt like both a gift and a curse. On the one hand, it gave me a great period of time to continue training my mind and more fully absorb the afterglow of my act of generosity. But on the other hand, it had been a *long* day by this point. I was sleepy after a big lunch at the temple, and I was almost guaranteed to hit traffic, which meant that internal battle that I went through on the way up was going to be equally, if not more, challenging on the way back. But I had been taught that recollecting your good deeds and training the mind to stay rooted in that proud, bright feeling can not only help you have a better, brighter mood, but it can also help you meditate and sleep better. And I don't know about you, but I was in need of all three of those things! With that in mind, I was determined to stay vigilant of my mind on the ride home.

But despite my desire to maintain this purity, the familiar thought patterns of that greed-based paradigm still made some strong appearances. Not long after making the donation, a thought would pop up: "Hmm, did I offer too much?" That sinking feeling of regret and doubt was so opposite in nature to the expansive, bright feeling of being proud of my generosity. But strangely enough, the mind just gets pulled back into these negative states like gravity. It's easy to dwell within such states for quite some time without even being aware of the shift. But after some time with the thoughts that accompanied the resurfacing of the greed-based paradigm, recognition and mindfulness of this shift arose. This was my opportunity to refocus my attention.

I would take a moment to release any disappointment as I, once again, compassionately reassured myself that this feeling was normal. Then I would instigate the shift by recollecting the things I was grateful for. How lucky was I to have a temple that was close enough to go to? "Some people want to talk to monks, support them, and receive the sacred blessings but simply don't have access to such things where they live. And even if people do have access, perhaps nobody has emphasized to them the practical training to help make each act of giving more fruitful! These teachings are helping me shift so deeply, and I am grateful for that." As my mind shifted back toward the brightness of my act of giving, I would rest it back in this proud feeling as long as I could.

As I continued this practice, what started out as just five, ten, or fifteen minutes of dwelling in that proud feeling turned into twenty. To Thirty. To an hour. To the whole trip! With consistent practice, my mind started to become accustomed to maintaining this mental brightness before, during, *and* after the act of giving. Instead of only feeling proud and happy at the moment of making the donation, the entire day became a joyful process that more deeply cleansed my mind.

However, this "after" phase is not just confined to the rest of that specific day when we perform the act of generosity. If we can train ourselves to connect with this proud feeling frequently, it can brighten our minds for many days, weeks, months, or years to come. It might even stick with us until the end of our life. This is why taking pictures, journaling, or even recording a voice note to capture the impact of the event in the moment or shortly afterwards can be incredibly helpful. These snapshots in time serve as gateways to help you more effectively and effortlessly reconnect with and stay rooted within the mental brightness that each act generates.

In fact, if we become adept at this stage and can habitually reconnect with that proud, bright feeling from our acts of giving, it's safe to say that this is the phase with the potential to create the most profound, comprehensive, and longest-lasting benefit in our lives. It will serve to not only improve our baseline mood in daily life but also prepare us to sleep more restfully, meditate more deeply, and even pass away in a more peaceful state.

Sleep, Meditation, and Death

I apologize for the sudden shift into something significantly less lighthearted in nature than properly tending to apple trees. However, in order to fully grasp the importance of cultivating the skills of recollection included in this "after" phase, it's imperative to clarify how it helps with not only our mood but also introduces a sense of ease into the process of sleep, meditation, and passing away peacefully at the moment of death. This may seem like an odd combination of topics, but these three sets of experiences do, in fact, share some interesting parallels that make them specifically relevant to this phase of giving. Each of these occurrences involve a process of letting go of our normal state of consciousness and transitioning into a completely new state. These transitionary processes can either be stressful or ease-filled based on how we approach them.

In the case of sleep, our body and mind must first be relaxed enough to slip into an unconscious state of rest. When people struggle to fall asleep, it often stems from the fact that they are unable to "turn off" their "thinking brain." Plans, worries, and stresses from the day or of what might happen in the future continue buzzing around within the mind, and we stay stuck in problem-solving mode. Using force and effort to stop thinking about such things at this point is typically ineffective or downright counterproductive.

Most of us are likely familiar with this feeling. Have you ever tried *very hard* to make yourself fall asleep? And how did that go? It was probably a frustrating night of tossing and turning until you finally released the effort out of exhaustion and fell into a restless sleep. Even that word alone—"falling"—points to the fact that sleep is a passive process where we must let go of control. When we can prepare the mind by properly recollecting our good deeds, it introduces a powerful pattern interrupt to our pre-sleep habits of thought and sets the conditions that prime the mind to let go more effectively. In other words, it facilitates a successful transition into a restful, rejuvenative sleep state.

Meditation is very similar. People often struggle with getting swept away in a torrent of thoughts riddled with negative emotions, yet if we try to "stop these thoughts" with force, we will have a very challenging and disappointing meditation session. Our awareness will continuously slip away from our grasp, and each instance of recognizing this wandering will further entrench us in aggravated tension. We might even just give up the practice of meditation entirely out of frustration and make the incorrect assumption that we are just inherently "not good at meditation."

The truth is, we simply need to adjust our approach. In addition to maintaining a gentle awareness and being in a relaxed physical state, our mind must be proficient at discovering and maintaining comfort and ease. And while there are many ways to do this that lie outside of the scope of this book, reconnecting with the positive energy from the good deeds we've done either before, in the middle, or at the end of our meditation is profoundly powerful when done correctly. This practice has been consistently reiterated by the most advanced meditators I have learned from as perhaps the number one key to deepening your meditation.

So, here are some tips to recollect effectively: In the case of both sleep and meditation, some people may find that reading a long description or mentally recapping their act of giving in detail is a bit too cognitive; it can actually fuel the mind's wandering and disrupt the process of falling asleep or meditating. It can be helpful to clarify that we are not necessarily trying to perfectly remember *all* of the details surrounding the acts. Rather, we are trying to reconnect with that warm, bright, fuzzy feeling that arose while performing the act. This is why journaling via pictures or having a few key words as a heading for each entry can be helpful. These brief verbal or visual summaries serve as a window into that warm, fuzzy state of mind.

To reiterate, this warm fuzziness speaks to the presence of spiritual energy—which, in Buddhism, we call merit. The "pure water" of merit is added to the mind not only when we give, but also when we meditate. It is what creates the purifying, blissful feeling that arises during good inner experiences. When we can effectively shift our mental state back into this feeling via lightly recollecting our good deeds, it sets the perfect conditions for the mind to let go of its typical tense wanderings and fall into a peaceful sleep or meditative state. For meditation specifically, this can either be done right before the start of the practice, in the middle when experiencing some strong mind wanderings, or at the end right before spreading loving kindness or forgiveness. You will be able to settle on what works best for you after some practice.

At first, recollecting this feeling may not feel fully natural. Our mind is not familiar with intentionally connecting with such feelings that often just arise at random, infrequent times when our heart is touched deeply by something that occurs in our lives. But now, we are cultivating a new skill. So if it feels a bit unnatural in the beginning, that is ok! This is why we use tools like journaling and taking pictures until the point where we can connect with that feeling more quickly, effortlessly, and deeply without needing to look at anything. If your mind wanders a bit more than you expect, that's also ok. As you practice fostering this connection before, during, and after your habit of generosity and as a supplement to sleep and meditation, you will become a pro in no time.

It's like walking to a point in the forest where you're surrounded by thick vegetation. Initially, walking to that point isn't so easy. There's no trail or recognizable landmarks nearby, and there are many obstacles in the way that can trip you up. But as you continue to walk this path consistently day after day, your footsteps begin to carve a more clearly defined path. You recognize each place to turn and what to avoid. The more consistently you walk this path, the easier and more natural it is to return to that point. You begin to know the way so well, you could do it with your eyes closed. Similar to how a river carves a deeper pathway into rock over time and gradually gains power and strength, your consistent practice will strengthen these new neural pathways to positivity powered by a growing catalog of good deeds. This will serve to root you more effortlessly in this mental brightness that will become your new normal. And as you practice, it will lead to a more cheerful baseline mood, more restful sleep, and more transformative meditation.

So, how does this prepare you for a peaceful passing at the moment of death? Well, back when I was a grievance counselor at a hospice, I noticed some patterns surrounding death. Regardless of the religious background or belief system held by the dying individual or the grieving family, all the loved ones and relatives who came to support and spend time with dying individuals universally sought to create a similar environment during their last moments. If any regrets or concerns came to mind, they would assure the dying individual that these things no longer mattered. They would encourage their loved one to forget such things and instead recollect the positive impact they had on others. They would recount the individual's good deeds and happy memories. They would settle into a calm quiet and gently hold this space of positivity.

Intuitively, everyone knows that a positive state of mind is important at the moment of one's death. And any time you hear accounts from people who have had near-death experiences, they typically say that their "lives flashed before their eyes." This process happens automatically—near the moment of death, the mind will naturally review the most prominent memories of our life. What we see is largely what we have habitually, whether intentionally or passively, allowed our mind to be occupied with. Perhaps the prompting of those around us—if we are lucky enough to pass in the presence of loved ones—can reconnect us with the good we've done, but it isn't certain that our mind will be lucid enough to follow such instructions. So, in such times when we don't have full control over our mind, our awareness will flow like water through the pathways that our mental habits have carved out over time and arrive at the most impactful moments that we can recall. If we have trained our mind properly—especially during transition states of sleep and meditation, when we similarly release active control of our awareness—then we can ensure that our mind is more prepared to let go in a way that allows for those pathways to lead us toward brightness.

Most people have an existential fear of death and, as a result, just don't want to think about these types of things. However, with wisdom, we can see that our death is inevitable. Although this fear of the unknown is understandable, it's important to balance this fear with wisdom. Instead of avoiding considering the inevitable and merely hoping and wishing that we will enter a positive and peaceful mind state when the time comes, we can adopt a wiser approach and actually practice for this moment. This consideration now elevates generosity training from a mere mood booster to a wise and tangible way to manage one of the most universal fears surrounding how to approach the inevitability and uncertainty of death. And since we never truly know when our time will come, it's best to stay prepared by practicing the concepts of this "after" phase every single day.

Now, let's take a moment to summarize some key ways we can recollect and reconnect with the purifying energy from each act of giving during the "after" phase. Firstly, much like in the "before" phase, it's important to remember that our mind is likely going to shift back into our familiar thought patterns of self-centeredness, doubt, or regret shortly after performing the act. And when it does, we can compassionately and consistently reconnect with gratitude and with the bright, positive mental state accompanied by the pure act of giving until it becomes more ingrained as a natural habit.

The next key point is that each act of giving can continue to brighten the mind even after that day of performing the act if we train our mind properly. Taking pictures and/or journaling and organizing these mementos from each act can serve as a powerful tool that helps us more easily reconnect with the bright, purifying energy from each act of giving. Revisiting this catalog of generosity, either mentally or by literally browsing the pictures or journal entries in a light fashion, can serve as a powerful way to prepare the mind for more effective and efficient meditation or sleep—or it can simply boost our mood when we need a pick-me-up.

Lastly, practicing recollection frequently until it becomes a deeply ingrained mental pattern ensures that our mind will flow more easily toward brightness, transition smoothly, and pass peacefully when the moment of our death arrives.

CHAPTER III
ADDRESSING FREQUENTLY ASKED QUESTIONS

Now that we have covered the main mechanism of how giving purifies the mind and how to unlock the full benefit of each act of generosity, let's address some frequently asked questions. After we clear up these commonly held doubts, you will have the confidence to dive right into the action plan that follows to help you implement a sustainable habit that works for your specific situation.

A Dollar a Day Keeps the Darkness Away

After hearing about all of these different types of giving and taking a closer look into my biweekly giving ritual, you might feel a bit overwhelmed or confused. We've covered so many different ways to give across a wide variety of contexts, scopes, and levels of complexity that now it might be a bit unclear where to start. What's most important? Is it sufficient to give every couple of weeks, or is there a sustainable way to give more frequently than this? Is it really necessary to give every day?

Ultimately, like any new habit that we want to successfully integrate into our lives, consistency is absolutely key. More large-scale acts of generosity like my biweekly donation, although very impactful for both giver and receiver, leave quite significant gaps of time between each act. These gaps allow for our existing greed-driven thought, speech, and behavior patterns that create the fabric of our daily awareness to continue to run on autopilot without much interruption. In the same way that eating healthy and doing a super intense workout at the gym once every two weeks will not effectively lead to losing belly fat and getting a perfectly cut six-pack, a truly effective transformation of the mind requires more consistency than just intermittent acts. What we require is a daily act of generosity. Then, and only then, will the habit be sure to stick within our lives and deeply shift the way we show up in the world.

In order to grasp how you might discover such a giving practice, I'd like to share the details of the daily practice I incorporated into my busy schedule even before becoming a monk. I was juggling many different professional, financial, and personal responsibilities at that time in my life. So in order to set myself up for success, I had to brainstorm to find a way to perform a daily act of generosity that didn't place an excessive financial burden on me or create a significant disruption of my daily schedule. As my first step to achieve this end, I found myself a nice jar. Next, I went to the bank and took out a big stack of one-dollar bills. Finally, I placed the jar and the cash on my bedside table right next to where I would meditate every morning. I now had all the raw materials and the appropriate setup necessary to perform my daily act of giving in a sustainable way.

In order to cultivate two daily habits that I intended to sustain for the rest of my life, I decided I would combine them into my own daily ritual that I incorporated into my morning routine. First, I would complete my task of meditating for at least five minutes shortly after waking up. Then, immediately after I was finished and my mind was still pure and bright from my daily "mind shower," I would take a dollar bill or two from the stack, place it in my palm as I put my hands in prayer position, and connect with my intention to release greed and support others with this donation. And finally, after making any wholesome resolutions, wishes, or prayers that I had for myself and others, I would place that dollar bill in the jar and move on to start the rest of my day.

This process continued for fourteen days. The jar would slowly fill up until it was time for me to take the daily donations and any additional money I wanted to give and drive up to the temple once every two weeks. Establishing this routine was a great way for me to create overlap between an act that I could easily perform every day and one that was more involved and deeply impactful that I could only perform on a more infrequent basis. This made my generosity training easier to coordinate and maintain over time.

Incorporating this daily meditation and giving ritual into my life that could take as little as about six to seven minutes allowed me to habitually dedicate time, energy, and resources to cultivating positive spiritual energy that would set a good tone for the rest of each and every day. And this practice, although seemingly small and insignificant, kept me consistently rooted in my intention to shift my paradigm, build a strong spiritual foundation, and take daily steps toward that better version of myself. I was progressively overcoming the heavy darkness from my past and generating a brightness of mind that spread throughout the rest of my daily life.

Of course, this is just one example that worked well for me. Although monetary donations do tend to be the most simple and accessible form of giving, there are many other ways to practice generosity daily, and you will have an opportunity to choose from a large list found in the next chapter. If another type of giving fits more sustainably into your daily schedule, feel free to choose whatever works best for you! Just keep in mind that in order for an act to be suitable for a daily practice, the time, energy, and resources required by the act should not place you in an unstable financial situation or interrupt your daily schedule too much. The act should also be very accessible; it should be something you will definitely have the opportunity to do every single day. When these characteristics are present, your practice of daily giving will be truly sustainable and deeply transformative.

Then, once you get the ball rolling on a daily practice, you can look toward something more involved and impactful, similar to my biweekly donation. You could even set your sights on something as grand and complex as a mission trip. Due to its complexity and the large investment of time, energy, and resources it requires, you might only do something like this once a year, or maybe even just once every few years. But since an act of this size gives you the opportunity to practice all of the steps we talked about in the last chapter over a long period of time, it will likely provide you with a life-altering experience with the power to uplift your mind with ease any time you think about it for many years to come. In other words, the high cost involved certainly also comes with a correspondingly significant positive impact on the mind.

As we start to gain confidence and reap the benefits of our generosity training, we can scale up to these larger acts if and when we feel called to do so, and these deeply impactful memories will certainly serve as strong fuel to brighten our minds into the future. However, our first priority is establishing a daily practice that will ensure that our generosity training sticks with us for the long haul!

The Magic of Spontaneity

Presented with all of these different categories of giving and structured ways of practicing them, you might be wondering: "Do I always have to plan everything out? Is it ok just to give more spontaneously?" Giving in a spontaneous fashion is commonly referred to as doing "random acts of kindness." Instead of being routine in nature and always taking the same form, we simply perform these acts when the opportunity presents itself. And yes, this type of giving is wonderful to practice and provides some unique advantages in comparison to more planned forms of giving.

The great thing about spontaneity—and why it's such a great supplement to more regimented giving—is that it can provide *unexpected* boosts of positive emotions for ourselves and others in daily life. Strangely enough, it also provides us with excellent opportunities to expose the various places in which greed shows up for us. When we perform a preplanned act of generosity, we've already considered a setting that resonates with us and have time to prepare our mind to be in a suitable state. However, if we keep the tenets of our generosity training in mind, we can also start to notice where we struggle with a reluctance to give or be generous with our time, energy, and resources throughout the day. These moments reveal where unwholesome patterns of thought, speech, and behavior have been running on autopilot, and they also reveal who and what situations give rise to such patterns. With this new awareness, we are further empowered to do the inner work necessary to show up as better versions of ourselves in the wide variety of situations we find ourselves in during daily life. To illustrate how this can actually become like a fun, exciting game of self-development, I'd like to share a story.

I have a friend in California—let's call her Terry. We shared this concept with Terry about how to practice generosity as a form of mind training, and she was ecstatic. It really resonated with her, and she went home inspired to start releasing greed from her mind. As she was going throughout her day, an opportunity for generosity training arose: In front of her on the countertop stood two big, juicy Minneola tangelos. What is that, you ask? Well, nothing other than a delightful cross between a tangerine and a grapefruit. Basically, it's an incredibly delicious orange that Terry liked more than any other fruit.

So, she asked her boyfriend if he wanted one and, of course, he said yes. As she picked up two oranges—one for herself and one for her boo—she was faced with a dilemma. One was clearly bigger and looked more tasty than the other. Obviously, that's the one Terry wanted. She laughed internally as she recognized that this was it . . . this was the moment she had been waiting for. Greed was manifesting in such a small instance where she was actually *already* practicing giving. Normally, Terry would have taken the large orange without a second thought, but this was a new Terry. And she was determined to make a change. So, with her hand slightly shaking with the effort required to release her attachment to her prized possession, she gave her boyfriend the bigger orange and ravenously ate the smaller one. By releasing her attachment to the sweetness of the bigger orange, she was able to enjoy the sweetness of that internal victory over greed.

Terry excitedly shared this story with our group when she returned for meditation class the following week, and everyone enjoyed the story as she recounted how difficult it was. She was so amazed at how she had never even realized before that moment how attached she was to food. Something so seemingly insignificant as having the bigger orange somehow had such a sway on her mind! But with her newfound awareness, she felt very proud of herself for winning this small internal battle that we all were able to appreciate and celebrate as a genuinely big step toward becoming aware of and overcoming greed in all of its forms.

Terry's story provides us with a good view into the powerful nature of spontaneous opportunities to give. Despite being so brief that we typically do not have enough awareness to notice them, this new perspective from our generosity-based paradigm can help us recognize situations where a reluctance to share our time, energy, or resources arises. Of course, there are times when we may be wisely protecting ourselves from dangerous or compromising situations, but there are certainly also moments when our patterns of greed are running on autopilot, and releasing them will lead to greater benefit for ourselves and others. We will cover how to differentiate between these two situations in a moment, but for now, just remember not to overlook the power of these random acts of kindness.

From Little, Give Little

Although we briefly discussed this earlier, it's important to emphasize that the amount you give is secondary to how well you train your mind to be bright and pure before, during, and after the act of giving. Sometimes people compare their own acts to those of others and feel that the amount they provide indicates an inferior action that isn't even valuable enough to perform. This simply is not the case! My meditation master always reiterates that the amount of spiritual energy generated depends most heavily on the quality of the giver's mind. Someone giving $1 with a purer intention and genuine joy receives far greater spiritual benefit than the individual who gives $100,000 while holding on to impure motives and experiencing a small amount of joy.

Always keep this in mind when undergoing your generosity training. There is no need to force yourself into an unsustainable practice for the sake of "keeping up" with those around you practicing generosity to a seemingly larger degree than you. The measure of success and impact is largely internal, so our attention should remain on our own process of releasing greed and cultivating brightness of mind. If you don't have much time, resources, or energy to spare, just give what you can sustainably manage in this moment. Work from where you are, not from where others are. Keep your eyes on your own process, and you will be able to give in a truly sustainable and purifying way.

Desire Isn't Always Greedy

Another topic people commonly wonder about is the concept of giving without expecting anything in return. Sometimes people will ask, "Since you get this positive spiritual energy when giving, is it greedy or selfish to give with the intention of gaining this in return?" It's important to note that the desire to train the mind, release unwholesome qualities, and cultivate wholesome qualities is not indicative of greed. Rather, this desire is itself wholesome in nature and should be cultivated instead of released. Such a positive internal motivation is the required fuel that drives one's life in a truly beneficial direction.

It's also important to note that gaining personal benefit from an action does not make it inherently selfish. In order for generosity training to be truly sustainable, it must create benefit for not only the receiver, but the giver as well. Otherwise, it is self-sacrificial, unsustainable, and ultimately unwise to engage in. Equally as important to understand is the fact that giving something beneficial and non-harmful to another always generates positive spiritual energy within the giver. This is just nature. The energy arises automatically.

So, because this positive spiritual energy is the purest benefit gained by the giver during an act of giving, you can rest assured that a desire to cultivate this energy via your generosity training is not selfish or greedy. In fact, the intention of practicing giving to gain more of this energy stands as an important characteristic of the ideal mindset we want to progressively work towards embodying, as this approach creates the best possible win-win scenario for both giver and receiver.

Next, let's dive into this concept of what a "pure" intention is and how to keep it at the forefront of your mind.

Patiently Cultivating a Purer Intention

A common topic that generosity practitioners have doubts about is the different motives people can have for giving. Once people start practicing more frequently, they will notice that the praise, validation, or reciprocation that comes from an act of giving actually feels quite good to them. That's when questions arise like: "If I enjoy these things, is that bad? If so, how do I let go of this attachment?"

To answer these questions, I would like to elaborate on an idea that we touched on briefly in the introduction—the reality that people give for a wide variety of reasons. We could categorize these reasons in a number of ways, but the list that follows will be pretty comprehensive. People will give:

- to return a favor that was done to them,
- to earn a favor from someone in the future,
- out of habit or simply to follow the example of others,
- due to social pressure or out of fear of disapproval or dislike from others,
- to be seen as generous by certain people,
- to look better than others around them,
- because they feel uplifted by the praise and attention,
- to lighten the burden of others,
- to train the mind to become pure and free from greed, or
- due to the joy and positive energy experienced when giving.

While there may be a few intentions for giving that are not explicitly covered in this list, the main point here is to highlight the fact that certain intentions for giving are more conducive than others to achieving the aims of this book: to give for the purpose of training the mind to release greed and cultivate generosity. Greed in this context not only refers to the attachment to the valuable item that we are offering to another—whether that's time, energy, or resources—but also the attachment to the *other* things that arise when we give. This could include the approval of others in the form of words, them merely holding us in higher regard, or reciprocation of the favor.

When we receive such benefits in return, it's only natural for us to enjoy them. After all, this is an indicator that the recipient is grateful, values our gift, and recognizes and welcomes our act of generosity. If it comes from observers of the act or people that we tell about it after the fact, it can also affirm that our generosity was a beneficial and commendable thing to do. And, just to be completely clear, it is ok and only natural to enjoy these external forms of validation to a certain degree as we start out with our generosity training!

These motivators are similar to using training wheels when we're first learning to ride a bike. In the beginning, they might be necessary to help instill our habit. We might seek out—either consciously or subconsciously—such praise and revel in it, because we haven't yet trained our internal sense of validation to be strong enough to sustain the practice on its own. We might notice that our mind only partially delights in helping others and undergoing generosity training and is more delighted by the praise, positive attention, or reciprocation given by others. And again, to reiterate, this is very normal in the beginning.

It is, however, helpful to keep in mind *why* it is beneficial for us to slowly but surely let go of such attachments. Although both parties still benefit from the act, attachment to this external validation interrupts the process of letting go of greed. We might develop a habit of *giving to get* as opposed to *giving to let go*. And if that praise is not present, shows up in a less pronounced manner, or doesn't come from the individual we hoped to get it from the most, we might end up feeling quite disappointed. This reaction reveals an overdependence on such things in order to feel joyful when giving, and as a result, the amount of positive spiritual energy we gain from the act is not as pronounced as it could be.

So, when we notice the presence of such attachments, we should simply become neutrally aware, allow for a few more moments of enjoyment from this validation, and then gently refocus our attention on our pure intentions for giving. Honoring where we are in this moment and slowly working toward the ideal state of mind is much more sustainable than harshly and abruptly chastising ourselves in our attempt to be perfect. Just like when the mind strays to thoughts of doubt, regret, or negativity for the before, during, and after phases, we just want to catch ourselves and refocus our attention back to those last three intentions on the list: to help others, to purify the mind of greed, and to brighten the mind with positive spiritual energy.

Bit by bit, as you train your mind to rest with those pure intentions, the attachment to receiving external validation will diminish and give rise to a much more fruitful, purifying act of giving. Then, when the praise or reciprocation comes, you can graciously and humbly accept it without actively seeking it out or becoming dependent on it in order to sustain or be truly joyful in your habit of giving.

Setting Wise Boundaries When Necessary

Now, with all of that being said, if the recipients of our giving make no indication that they are grateful or appreciate it, do we still have to keep giving to them? What if they actually berate or criticize our efforts? Or what if they seem to be taking advantage of our generosity? How do we protect ourselves from such situations?

Since we just talked about how it's helpful to detach from positive responses from people after an act of giving, now let's address how to deal with a lack of response or ones that are negative in nature. It's true that we certainly do want to train our mind to detach from external validation and have brightness and joy arise from within. However, this doesn't necessarily mean that we have to endure situations that compromise our own emotional well-being.

In the same way that we want to give an amount that does not financially deplete us, we should also try to implement this practice of habitual giving with a recipient who does not emotionally deplete us. Now wait—before you stop giving time and energy to your children or significant others when they get on your nerves and tell them the Buddhist monk told you to do so, let's clarify what that means for a second! Many of us have responsibilities toward those who are dependent upon or have a close relationship to us, and we have surely been giving to them before even reading this book. With these individuals, you can still work on giving with a more joyful mind even if they don't fully recognize or appreciate your efforts.

Mundane tasks or acts of kindness—like giving them the last cookie, washing their dishes, or spending time supporting them when they feel down—become more beneficial to both giver and receiver when we practice the concepts of cultivating joy before, during, and after. These acts are not grand, official, or out of the ordinary, so they might not be fully appreciated or could even go unnoticed at times by those closest to us. It certainly can be helpful to calmly share with the individual how you both can make sure each other feels appreciated through your words and actions, but that's a rabbit hole of healthy communication tips that certainly lies outside of the scope of this book.

The main point here is: When we can reframe the situation to understand how such acts can still brighten our mind, we can conduct these tasks with more frequency and joy without being too attached to an enthusiastic response from those we love. This allows for us to give joyfully in a more spontaneous way on top of our regimented daily habit of giving, thus further supporting the release of a greed-based paradigm and fostering the firm establishment of a generosity-based one. As long as we balance caring for others with an appropriate amount of self-care, such selfless giving is sustainable and will definitely have a positive effect on our relationships in addition to positively affecting our own mind.

So then the question becomes: How do we deal with an act of giving to an organization or person outside of our close circle who responds in an unappreciative or negative fashion? Or what if there are some strong indications that this person or organization is taking advantage of our generosity? Maybe they seem to be manipulating us or pressuring us into giving more than we are willing to. Experiencing such situations can be disheartening and may make us doubt the fact that giving is even a wise thing to do in a world where people are mostly just looking out for themselves.

And the reality is, sometimes our acts may *not* be fully appreciated. Perhaps they might be misunderstood as us trying to gain favor or signaling that we're more virtuous than others. People might criticize and question our intentions. Maybe the recipient displays a lack of contentment and pressures us to donate or offer more than we are able.

In some professional or competitive situations, giving freely to others may not be fully appropriate or in line with the culture; in others, the recipient may be seeking to actively take advantage of our generosity via manipulative, high-pressure tactics. When a feeling of obligation becomes the driver of our actions or the amount that we give, negative feelings of doubt and guilt can arise, which are directly oppositional in nature to the brightness of mind we seek to cultivate. It's important for us to recognize that these contexts are not so supportive for the purposes of effective generosity training. So, when we encounter such situations, we must set wise boundaries to protect ourselves and just find another setting where giving is safe, appropriate, and appreciated. This will help us feel secure in the knowledge that the recipient cares about us and is not pressuring us into compromising situations, allowing us to continue building up our spiritual foundation in a context that is more supportive of our aims.

CHAPTER IV
ACTION PLAN

Now, we have officially made it to the most exciting part of this book! It's time to take everything that we've learned so far and make a plan of action in order to sustainably implement a habitual practice of giving into your life. This chapter is going to help you produce a personalized map to success that you can continuously reference as you cultivate and strengthen this habit. This chapter is very interactive and engaging, so please enjoy the process!

I'm very excited for you to identify your own way of giving that is both deeply healing and truly sustainable for you and your situation. To start, let's take a look at a how we will create this plan:

1. Identify the acts of giving that intrigue you
2. Pick one act of generosity to perform
3. Choose where you will perform this act
4. Decide what time of day you will perform this act
5. Decide how much you will give (i.e., a dollar amount, time duration, or amount of resource)
6. Prepare or buy any needed supplies
7-9. Give in the most healing way in each phase: before, during, and after
10. Adjust and repeat
11. Invite others to join you

Step 1: Identify the Acts of Giving That Intrigue You

It's now time to take a look at the long list of potential ways to give and make note of which ones intrigue or excite you. This process will help you narrow down the myriad ways that you can practice generosity into a more approachable, manageable list of activities that you feel drawn to. The list below will provide specific examples from each type of giving that we've covered in previous chapters. Although there are certainly ways to give that are not explicitly stated in this list, it should help you find a great starting place to begin your journey.

As you scan through the list below, observe your initial reaction as you read each bullet point. If you feel a jolt of excitement, then mark that action down in your notes to add to your own list. Reading this list might even spark a totally different idea of how you could give that is not explicitly stated in this book—go ahead and jot those ideas down as well! You are also welcome to simply highlight or underline directly in the book on your first read-through and then organize the acts electronically or on paper afterwards. Do whatever is most convenient for you.

Just remember as you read that you're not making any commitments at this point, so there's no need to overthink it or doubt if you will actually enjoy this type of giving. Just go with your initial gut feeling, and either write down or highlight the options that speak to you or skip over the ones that don't. Once you have completed this part of the action plan, you will be equipped with a more condensed list that we will work with further in the coming steps.

Go ahead and get ready to make some notes on a sheet of paper, a note on your electronic device, or in this book, and then start reading through the list below. Have fun with this activity, and get excited with the recognition that you are discovering specific, enjoyable ways of giving that will deeply shift your life!

Gifts or Donations of Money

To Organizations:

- Donate to a local food bank.
- Donate to an international disaster relief organization.
- Donate to an animal shelter.
- Donate to a local art museum.
- Support a community theater.
- Contribute to a music school.
- Donate to a children's hospital.
- Contribute to a cancer research fund.
- Fund a medical clinic.

- Contribute to a scholarship fund.
- Donate to a public school.
- Donate to a literacy program.
- Support your local church.
- Support a temple or spiritual organization.
- Donate to a meditation center.
- Donate to a housing organization.
- Help fund a neighborhood revitalization project.
- Give financial support to a community garden initiative.
- Donate to a microfinance organization.
- Contribute to a crowdfunding campaign.
- Contribute to a skills development program to help job seekers acquire new skills.

To Individuals:

- Give money to a homeless person.
- Pay for the coffee or meal of the person behind you in the drive-through.
- Pay for part or all of your friend's tank of gas.
- Offer a cash gift to a friend or family member struggling with their finances.
- Help with a friend or family member's tuition.
- Fund a scholarship to support a first-generation college student.
- Donate to a family or individual affected by a natural disaster.
- Donate for general expenses of a respected religious/spiritual figure.
- Contribute to a spiritual/religious leader spearheading helpful programs.
- Help fund an entrepreneur starting a small business.
- Provide financial assistance to a family in need.
- Give money to a family facing unexpected medical bills.
- Support a grieving family to help cover funeral costs.
- Give to a memorial fund creating a positive impact in memory of a lost loved one.

- Fund the adoption process to help a family bring a child home.
- Donate to an elderly neighbor to assist with home care services.
- Sponsor a vocational training course for an unemployed individual.

Donating, Sharing, or Gifting Physical Items

To Organizations:

- Provide gently used clothing to a local shelter for those in need.
- Donate blankets to a nonprofit helping the homeless during winter.
- Give business attire to an organization assisting job seekers.
- Offer grocery store gift cards to a food bank to help struggling families.
- Give gas station gift cards to a charity helping with transportation.
- Donate meditation cushions and supplies to a monastery.
- Offer robes, food, shelter, or medicine to monks and nuns.
- Provide food or necessities to a spiritual/religious community.
- Donate building materials to an organization constructing homes for the less fortunate.
- Offer sewing machines and fabric to a community craft center.
- Provide tools or equipment to a vocational training program.
- Give computers or laptops to a school for underserved students.
- Donate tablets for a digital literacy program for seniors.
- Donate a used car to a charity helping low-income families.
- Provide a van to a nonprofit transporting individuals with disabilities.
- Offer textbooks to a community library or school.
- Donate children's books to a literacy program for kids.
- Provide educational resources to a nonprofit promoting learning.

- Contribute medical supplies to a clinic in need.
- Provide medical equipment to an organization aiding disaster relief efforts.
- Give toys or games to a children's hospital for young patients.
- Donate board games to a youth center for recreational activities.
- Donate stuffed animals to comfort children in crisis situations.
- Support an art therapy program with donations of paints and brushes.
- Provide art supplies to schools.
- Donate crafting materials to an organization serving the elderly.
- Donate toiletries or personal care items to a homeless shelter.
- Provide feminine hygiene products to support disadvantaged women.
- Donate diapers or baby wipes to a family assistance program.
- Offer furniture to a housing organization for families transitioning out of homelessness.
- Give sports gear to a youth sports program for underprivileged children.
- Support a back-to-school drive with donations of backpacks and supplies.
- Provide calculators and educational materials to a tutoring program.
- Contribute pots, pans, or utensils to a homeless shelter's kitchen.
- Provide cookware or appliances to a community center.
- Donate formula or baby food to a family support program.
- Provide cribs or baby gear to an organization aiding new parents.
- Set up a table and provide refreshments for volunteers during a community service project.

To Individuals:

- Give the bigger, more delicious-looking piece of food to your friend or family member.
- Allow someone in a hurry to take your place in line at a store.
- Write a note of appreciation or motivation to a friend or family member.
- Hold the door open for a stranger.
- Share a warm coat with a friend in need during the winter.
- Offer freshly baked cookies or another homemade dish to welcome a new neighbor.
- Surprise a child with a new toy for their birthday.
- Gift a favorite book to a colleague who loves reading.
- Share art supplies with a creative friend for their project.
- Give an old smartphone to a family member who needs one.
- Make a playlist for a friend.
- Lend your tools to a neighbor for their home improvement project.
- Gift homegrown vegetables from your garden to a local senior.
- Share extra pet food or treats with a friend who has a furry companion.
- Offer fitness equipment to a friend who wants to start working out.
- Pass on a gently worn sweater to a family member who admires it.
- Share a stylish accessory with a friend for a special occasion.
- Share extra produce from your garden with neighbors.
- Hand down cherished childhood toys to younger relatives.
- Give electronics that you don't use much to someone in need.
- Share a rare vinyl record with a music enthusiast.
- Give a concert ticket to a fellow fan of the artist.
- Provide restaurant vouchers to someone in need.
- Buy a coworker a cup of coffee.

Volunteering Your Time, Labor, Energy, and Skills

To Organizations:

- Participate in a community cleanup by picking up litter in a local park.
- Join a neighborhood watch program to help keep your local community safe.
- Volunteer at a soup kitchen to serve meals to those in need.
- Volunteer your tutoring services to an organization that helps students struggling with their studies.
- Help build and repair homes with a nonprofit housing or disaster relief organization.
- Volunteer at a hospital to assist with patient care and support.
- Help an environmental conservation organization plant trees.
- Join a disaster relief team to aid in emergency response efforts.
- Volunteer at an animal shelter to care for and find homes for animals.
- Assist in elderly care by visiting and helping seniors with daily tasks.
- Mentor youth in after-school programs to provide guidance and support.
- Share your technical expertise by providing free consultation to local organizations or nonprofits.
- Go on a mission trip to provide aid to underserved communities either domestically or abroad.

To Individuals:

- Make a meal for someone, especially during a difficult time.
- Assist with packing and unpacking during a move of residence.
- Offer to babysit children to give their parents a break.
- Cook and share a meal with individuals who are extra busy.

- Give free lessons to help someone learning a new language.
- Provide tech support to troubleshoot issues with electronics.
- Lend a listening ear to let someone vent and process emotions during a difficult time.
- Complete someone's household chores or errands.
- Collaborate on DIY projects to tackle home improvements together.
- Help with gardening tasks such as weeding or planting flowers.
- Review and improve someone's resume or CV for job applications.
- Offer support and motivation to someone as a workout partner.
- Share a smile and positive energy to brighten others' days.

Sharing Wisdom

- Share inspirational wisdom quotes and reflections on social media.
- Share wise habits that you have developed and how they have helped you with friends.
- Engage in informal discussions about wisdom principles and teachings.
- Offer your time and encouragement to those seeking guidance on their spiritual path.
- Recommend wisdom books and resources for self-study, personal development, and spiritual exploration.
- Make donations to support organizations that spread wisdom in some capacity.
- Provide assistance to friends interested in starting their meditation practice.
- Organize book clubs to collectively study and discuss wisdom literature.
- Create or join meditation groups to practice and learn together.
- Write blog posts or articles sharing your wisdom experiences and insights.
- Organize a weekend retreat for participants to meditate and explore and discuss timeless

wisdom and life principles.

- Form a study group to delve into wisdom texts and foster discussions on moral and ethical values.
- Create a YouTube channel to offer video lessons on personal development and well-being.
- Gift a copy of classic literature on wisdom to a friend interested in personal development.
- Express wisdom themes through artistic endeavors like painting, drawing, graphic design, or writing.
- Arrange public exhibitions on Buddhist art and culture.
- Host online wisdom discussions and forums for a broader audience.
- Collaborate with other practitioners to create multimedia wisdom resources.
- Organize public lectures on religious or philosophical principles and ethics.
- Develop meditation apps or software for digital wisdom practice.
- Translate wisdom texts into different languages for wider accessibility.
- Publicly share your writings on wisdom within your field of expertise.
- Organize interfaith dialogues and discussions to promote understanding.
- Lead pilgrimages to sacred sites of significance.

Giving or Asking for Forgiveness

Mentally While Alone

- Mentally ask for forgiveness from anyone you have hurt, whether with or without your knowledge, recollection, or intention. Perform this mental task after meditation, while praying, or simply when you are sitting in quiet reflection.
- Mentally offer forgiveness to those who have harmed you after meditation, while praying, or simply when you

are sitting in quiet reflection. Stay consistent until it feels truly heartfelt.

Verbally With Another Person

- Call or meet up with someone you have hurt to fully own up to your wrongs and humbly apologize for the harm you caused.

- If someone has offered an apology that you previously rejected, either call or meet up to share that you have forgiven them.

Step 2: Pick One Act of Giving to Perform

Now that you have selected some items from the lists above and have written down any of your own unique acts of generosity that came up as you read, it's time to get even more specific. In this section, you will identify which act to perform first as you start off with your generosity training. As you read the items on your own list, imagine yourself completing this task. How will it feel? Take note of which act seems like it will be the most heartwarming and engaging as you visualize performing it.

Another important consideration is whether the act is suitable for you to perform with daily consistency. As stated earlier, daily practice is essential to ensure that the habit is truly transformational and sticks within your life for the long term. So, as you're first starting out with your generosity training, it's best to aim for those low-hanging fruits and select an act that is both simple and easily achievable for you. This will ensure that the difficulty of the act doesn't stand in the way of you getting started.

If you feel a strong calling to an act that requires a significant time, resource, or energy investment, then you can set that act as a goal for the near future. But if there is synergy between a simpler act and a larger one—for example, putting money in a jar every day until donating the entire amount to an organization in a few weeks' time—then you can choose the daily contribution as the first act you will perform. This way, you can still honor what resonates with you most while fulfilling the primary purpose of this section: to identify an act that is simple enough to sustainably complete on a daily basis into the future.

Let's address one last side note regarding forgiveness before moving on: If you decide to incorporate sharing and asking for forgiveness into your daily life, make sure that you incorporate some other act of giving alongside this practice. For the purposes of this book, we want to make sure that we are doing something every day that specifically releases greed and cultivates generosity, not just releases anger and cultivates loving kindness. This is not to downplay the latter; rather, we just want to make sure that the daily habit we cultivate functions primarily as an antidote to greed.

So, with that being said, go ahead and grab your writing utensil or electronic device and make a note of which act resonates the most with you from your list. If you're having trouble settling on one between three or four acts, just make note of all of them and pick the one that will be easiest to complete. Again, taking action is the most important thing! You can always adjust and try the other actions on your list after you complete your first round of generosity training.

Steps 3–6: Logistical Decisions and Preparations

Now that you have identified the act that you will perform, it's time to make a few simple decisions and clarify and complete any logistical steps involved in your act of giving. Take a moment now to plug in the appropriate answers to the following questions by either writing them on a separate sheet of paper, writing directly in the book, or just making a mental note.

- Where will I perform this act?
- What time will I perform this act?
- How much will I give (i.e., a dollar amount, time duration, or amount of resource)?
- What supplies do I need to get or preparations do I need to make?

Once you have answered these questions, go ahead and complete any preparation work that you have identified.

Steps 7–9: Give in the Most Healing Way

Now that you are 100 percent prepared for your act of giving, it's time to apply everything you've learned and undergo your first round of generosity training! These three steps of the action plan will recap the essence of how to give in the most healing way as well as cover the actions you can take to maximize the purifying effect of each act for the before, during, and after phases. Any actionable item on this to-do list that is marked "Optional" is not mandatory and can be omitted if you feel that it is too burdensome, time-consuming, or simply doesn't resonate with you.

Once again, remember that getting started and continuing to give every single day is the absolute most important thing. That is why the habit tracker—a simple and incredibly powerful way to feel proud of and stay consistent with a habit—is highly recommended as an additional resource. Once you build up your momentum, you can scale up and begin doing every step for each phase if you are so inclined. The actions for the "after" phase stand as some of the most powerful ways to deeply integrate the lasting benefits from these acts of giving into your daily life. So once you feel more stable and confident in your habit, incorporating these actions will serve to shift your life all the more deeply.

Without further ado, let's get into how you can give in the most healing way.

Before the Act

- Neutrally notice thoughts of doubt, complaints, and negativity as they arise. Take a moment to remind yourself that this is normal and natural, then kindly and gently reconnect with your pure intentions and the positive effects generated by the act.
    - ° This step starts at this phase and should be practiced as continuously as possible for the entirety of the other phases as well.
- (Optional) Right before you are about to give, close your eyes and meditate for a minute (or even longer) to bring the mind to a peaceful state of presence. This will help to maximize the depth of inner transformation and the spiritual energy you will cultivate.

During the Act

- Perform the act of giving while maintaining your mind in the way detailed above.
- (Optional) If appropriate, take a picture or have someone else take one to help you recollect this moment.
- (Optional) Make positive wishes or prayers for yourself, the recipient, or the ones you love as you perform the act.
  - ° When you perform an act of generosity, that is a powerful time to harness the positive spiritual energy that has just arisen and make a wish, resolution, or prayer to guide your life or the lives of others in a positive direction.

After the Act

- (Highly Recommended) Make a mark on your habit tracker.
  - ° Connect with that proud feeling of accomplishment each time you tick off your giving habit for a day.
  - ° Three sample habit trackers can be found in the Accountability Resources section or printed via the link in the footnote.[1]
- (Optional) Capture the feeling you're experiencing shortly after giving.
  - ° You can utilize pictures, journaling, videos, voice memos, etc.
  - ° You can journal either on your phone or in a physical journal.
  - ° Printable journal templates can be found on our website or in the Accountability Resources section.
- (Optional) Return to your journal entries each night or simply

---

1 https://nickkeomahavong.com/giving

mentally recap your acts of generosity as part of your routine to fall asleep more peacefully.

- (Optional) Reconnect with the bright feeling from your acts of giving to help your meditation sessions.
    - ° You can recollect before, during, or after the meditation session based on what works best for you.
- (Optional) Return to your journal whenever you need a pick-me-up.
    - ° Whenever you are having a difficult time, this can give you a powerful anchor to refocus your attention on that bright, positive feeling you have earned through your actions.

Step 10: Adjust and Repeat

Congratulations! Now that you have successfully completed your act of generosity and taken the steps to derive even more brightness of mind from it after the fact, it is time to review each previous stage, make any necessary adjustments, and repeat the process. Once you discover where improvements can be made, you can then make appropriate adjustments to make the giving process smoother and even more joyful moving forward. Similar to how it takes time to become skilled at a new sport or hobby, this process of trial and error is simply a natural part of the journey. So if the first round or two feel a bit awkward or clunky, just know that it will become smoother and easier over time as you discover your own rhythm and hone in on a way of giving that works best for you.

The following list of questions will guide this process of reviewing your acts of giving to discover how everything went and what adjustments can be made. Feel free to write down your answers so that you have a clear grasp of where improvements can be made for next time, or if this feels like too much work at this stage, you can simply read the questions and make a mental note for the next time you complete your act.

- Were you fully prepared for your act of giving? If not, what other preparations might be helpful?
- Did the amount of time, money, or resources that you gave feel like too much, too little, or just right in order to both feel proud and be sustainable for you to give consistently? If it was too much or too little, how can you adjust?
- Was the time of day appropriate? If not, what other time frame might work?
- Did you resonate with the specific type of giving you conducted? If not, feel free to revisit your list and try a completely new act or give to a new recipient.
- What did you do as a "pregame ritual" for your act of giving? Was it effective at helping you enjoy the process and preparing your mind properly for the act? If not, what might you do differently?
- Was there anything that you did for the "after" phase of giving that was very effective at helping you to reconnect with that proud, bright feeling?
- What else stands out to you as a way that you can make the act more seamless and enjoyable?

Once you have answered these questions and identified potential areas for improvement, you can then make a plan of how to proceed with your habit of giving. If you feel confident and want to start scaling up into larger acts of giving to complete a bit more sporadically in addition to this daily habit, you can run through all of the steps of this action plan to help with that new act as well.

Step 11: Invite Others to Join You

This final step adds an additional social component to your wholesome habit that can greatly enrich your generosity training. As a quick disclaimer, it is advisable to become strong and confident within your own practice first before extending any invitations for others to join you. Having a decent amount of experience will allow you to both identify what acts of giving you enjoy the most and clearly explain the benefits you've experienced to others. In addition, it will ensure that any objections that happen to arise from the people you invite won't cause you to doubt the value of continuing your own personal practice; in this case, the positive benefits you've experienced will outweigh their own opinions.

Once your habit is quite stable and you feel confident in it, inviting family and friends can add another level of enjoyment to your generosity training. This provides a great way to bond over a wholesome activity, and it can open up the possibility for mutual support as you keep each other accountable. Volunteer projects run by organizations can be a great option for this collaborative giving, as they are specifically designed for and warmly welcome as many helping hands as possible. At the very least, they can certainly be great places to connect with like-minded individuals you can create spiritual friendships with. Regardless of how you go about it, it can be incredibly enriching to grow into a better version of yourself alongside someone you care about!

CONCLUSION

Reactions to the Current State of the World

Since you have now properly mapped out your own personalized action plan to successfully implement your habitual generosity training into your life, it's almost time to release you on your path of transformation. But before we do so, let's talk about the current state of the world and the large-scale issues that we all are facing. I know what you might be thinking . . . "Yikes! That doesn't sound like a very fun, inspiring way to end this book!" But just hear me out for a second! Hopefully, it will be exactly that and much more.

If we keep up with global issues to any degree, the future might look pretty grim—maybe even downright apocalyptic. Violent conflicts and wars, serious economic crises, complex environmental issues, deep social divisions, the outbreak of diseases, corrupt leadership and governance, and countless atrocities against humanity seem so prevalent that it's completely unsurprising when anything new along these lines comes to light. On top of this, there's also a prevailing uncertainty about whether or not the information provided on these topics is even accurate or transparent. Media outlets tend to present this information in a sensationalized way in order to create a more enraged and, consequently, more engaged audience. We are constantly bombarded by this information that identifies and blames "the bad guys"—who are dangerous and not to be trusted—as the root cause of the issue at hand. As a result, we become ensnared by the idea that if we can only defeat or eradicate such "bad guys," everything will suddenly be better.

Armed with such ideologies, some people identify the issues that are most upsetting or negatively impactful for them and put in immense effort to fight against them. They'll take up arms on social media, engage in heated debates, or even take to the streets and protest the identified cause of the issue. Maybe they'll join or create a group of people seeking to push for the same type of change. Meanwhile, others might just turn a blind eye to these large-scale conflicts and stay focused on their own personal life, and some people lie somewhere in between these two sides of the spectrum. Honestly, any approach is understandable.

On the one hand, these issues *are* scary, and they can often have a direct and palpable impact on our lives. This is precisely why doing *something* feels better than doing nothing. And beyond that, it's important to appreciate that we can create positive impacts when we raise a passionate voice, take decisive action, and bring awareness to things that might be overlooked by the masses.

However, even with the best of intentions, a high level of intelligence, and plenty of other relevant skills, stepping into any situation in an emotionally charged state of mind can often lead to us unwittingly stoking the flames of conflict. Forcefully uprooting and overcoming current unjust scenarios often creates a distinct winner and loser, and this approach leads to an "us vs. them" mentality that opens up a drive for retribution, thus instigating a power struggle that fuels a never-ending cycle of conflict. Even if our efforts are successful at solving one issue, it's easy for a whole new set of unintended problems to be left in its wake.

And so, in light of the danger and complexity of combatting large-scale issues, some people simply choose to focus on themselves. And again, this approach is understandable—life is tough. There's a lot of problems to deal with, and sometimes we have so many responsibilities to juggle that it's hard to even keep our head above water. Our plates can become so full that there is simply no spare bandwidth to consider such seemingly insurmountable issues. In order to stay afloat and not succumb to a feeling of utter hopelessness and powerlessness, we might just choose not to pay much attention to these large-scale issues.

The Real Enemy

So, then, is it a "damned if we do, damned if we don't" situation? Not quite. I would like to propose an alternative approach that honors people with aims of either solely overcoming their personal issues or tackling large-scale issues in tandem. But before I do so, the most important thing is to clarify where the *deepest root cause* of *every single one* of these large-scale problems actually lies. Otherwise, if we fail to identify the root, our efforts are akin to chopping off the stem and leaves of a large weed. It still takes a lot of work and might be effective to a certain degree, but a complex root system is still present underneath the surface. Before long, the same problem will show up once more. It may take on a different form, but it is absolutely certain to arise again.

So, what is the root cause of the issue? Despite the vast number of differences and complexities in the myriad conflicts we face across the globe, every single one of them—without exception—has its origin within the human mind. All conflict—from the level of the individual to the household, the community, the country, or the international level all the way up to the global scale—always arises as a result of greed, anger, and delusion within the minds of partic-ipating parties. These are the driving forces that generate thinking, speaking, and behaving with a surplus of self-interest and emotion, a deficit of empathy and patience, and an absence of wisdom and clarity. Compound enough interpersonal conflict and soon enough, local conflicts escalate to reach the global scale.

The main takeaway here is that conflict on a macro scale is simply a reflection of what is happening on the micro scale. What is happening within the world is merely a reflection of what is happening within the mind. With this understanding of the problem, we are empowered to overcome it in a more effective way. And luckily for us, the wisdom from the monastery that illuminates the nature of the mind, the way it gets polluted by the outside world, and how to overcome such mental pollution to see things clearly has never been so readily available.

This path of training the mind to overcome darkness and cultivate brightness is no longer confined only to those willing to give everything up, seek out a sage deep within the forest of an exotic land, and practice these teachings in isolation. It is available here, now, right at your fingertips. It is achievable regardless of your current situation. And this path of inner work—that most often overlook or are unaware of—holds the key to how people with aspirations of mere personal development or aims of instigating change on a much larger scale can do so more effectively.

Light Your Own Candle and Pass It On

To wrap up this book, I'd like to tell you one last story. In our travels around the world, we've had the opportunity to run and take part in many candlelight meditation events, and some of these have included *thousands* of candles spread throughout an expansive event space. After some introductions and other opening segments, the time would arrive when it was necessary to light all of the candles in a safe, quick, and peaceful way. There is simply no way we would have been able to accomplish our task in a reasonable amount of time if we left it solely up to the twenty or so volunteers in attendance. So, we used a different approach.

Our volunteers started by lighting their own candles first. Then they made their way to help the people at the edge of each row light their candles. Once successfully lit, every person would then pass that flame onwards to the next individual while the volunteers took care of the candles farther away from the seating area. Each candle throughout the event was lit with speed and coordination, and soon the entire event space was illuminated by the warm glow of candlelight.

So how does this apply to our situation? Well, I personally like to see each of us as a candle, and our job in this lifetime is to do the work to ignite our own flame. Then, when you walk into a room after having taken the time to do this, you just shine. You don't even have to say much—there is just something unique about you. The way you carry yourself. The warmth of your smile. The sparkle in your eyes. It's magnetic. The people around you can't quite put a finger on it, but you are palpably different from the vast majority of people. You possess an inner quality that is rare in today's world.

What they are seeing—that perhaps they can't even articulate—is that you have lit your own candle of goodness inside of yourself. And what it sparks is a recognition. A recognition that they have that latent goodness inside of themselves, too. It inspires them to follow suit to try to cultivate that same internal luster and light *their* own inner candle. And maybe they will even ask you outright, "How is it that you're able to remain so genuinely cheerful? How are you so patient and peaceful despite being in stressful situations? How are you so kind and giving even when others around you aren't?" And this opens up an opportunity to share how you've been training yourself and potentially instigates the beginning of a beautiful, mutually supportive spiritual friendship with that person.

But even if they don't explicitly state it or ask how you did it, the way that you show up introduces a pattern interrupt from the norm and sparks a bit of hope for humanity within their mind. The impact your inner work has on others is especially impactful when you show up as a different version of yourself to people who have known you for a while. You lead by example and embody a model that proves that people *can*—and do—let go of deep-seated, unhealthy patterns and change for the better. Your close acquaintances see you as a testament to the fact that they, too, can change. You not only reinstate a faith in humanity within their minds, but you also inspire a faith that a kinder, more generous, and effortlessly cheerful version of themselves is genuinely achievable if only they have the courage to walk the path that you've undertaken.

And if, in fact, we are in a position where we are capable of and drawn toward actively pushing for change on a larger scale than our personal lives, let's take inspiration from the example of some of the most effective agents of change in the past. Mahatma Gandhi's famous quote pleaded for people to "be the change you wish to see in the world." Gandhi's message was so powerful and effective precisely because it was so unique during that tumultuous time period in Indian history. The power he wielded was the ability to face egregious displays of greed, anger, and delusion on a large scale with selflessness, patience, loving kindness, and wisdom. This is not a typical response at all and displays his possession of a power that originated from within. Instead of demonizing the forces of oppression by fighting anger with anger, violence with violence, greed with greed, and fire with fire, he quelled those fires within his own mind first. And then once Ghandi took to the streets and voiced his opinions—peacefully, without any initial prominent position of authority—he inspired the masses and changed the course of history forever.

Nowadays, there are countless people *talking* about needed changes in the world and a deficit of people really *becoming* that change. Talk is cheap. Instead of just talking about peace, wisdom, understanding, forgiveness, the need of others to give more, and the need for some group outside of ourselves to change, let us collectively commit to doing the work to *become* peaceful. To *become* wise and understanding. To work toward forgiveness and give with an open heart. To *become the change we wish to see in the world.*

When we do this, we lead by example and avoid hypocrisy. When we do this, our words—now backed by an embodiment of what we preach—become so much more powerful. This inner work helps us develop the rare ability to patiently and peacefully hold space for opposing viewpoints, listen with genuine empathy and a desire to understand, and communicate and act in a way that builds bridges that connect instead of walls that divide. As a result, we ensure that our efforts to make a positive impact on our immediate circles—or even circles much larger than that, if we so desire—create genuine benefit and truly reduce suffering for ourselves and for others instead of unwittingly contributing to the problem. And as our internal power grows with our continued triumph over the greed, anger, and delusion within our own minds, our spheres of positive influence will only continue to grow.

We will show up in all of the important roles and contexts that we find ourselves in, both professional and personal, as better versions of ourselves. As we become true practitioners of goodness and habitually train the mind accordingly, what we think, say, and do will come into harmonious alignment, and *our life will become our message.* This congruence of our being will inspire others, and that flame of inner brightness will soon spread to our family, our community, our country, and the world at large. In the same way that the global interconnectedness facilitated by modern technology can amplify and spread darkness much more quickly than ever before, luckily, it can do the same with light and wisdom.

In writing this guide, my sincerest hope is that you begin to see the gravity of the situation and understand how much power you already hold within you to improve your own life and the world around you when you focus your effort and energy in the right place. This is truly our only hope if we are to overcome the deep conflict we see on full display across the globe, because as Dr. Martin Luther King, Jr. once famously said, "Darkness cannot drive out darkness; only light can do that. Hate cannot drive out hate; only love can do that."

Similarly, greed cannot drive out greed; only generosity can do that. You are now equipped with all the practical steps you need to succeed in instigating that internal shift and becoming that agent of change. The time has come—the candle has now been passed on to you. The only question that remains is this: Are you ready to accept the flame? Ultimately, the choice is yours. Will you join us as we collectively do the work to defeat the enemy within and make this world a brighter place? We certainly hope so. The world is waiting on someone like you to recognize and ignite your internal source of power and become a shining beacon of hope for humanity.

Thank you for reading, and I wish you the best of luck on your journey. We'll see you again soon in the next book.

BLESSING

May you be happy, healthy, wealthy, and well-balanced in all areas of your life. May you successfully discover and implement a transformational habit of giving that continuously uproots a greed-based paradigm and cultivates a genuine paradigm of generosity. May you find deep enjoyment in being of service to others and discover contentment and gratitude within the life you live. May you and your loved ones be protected from all harm, danger, and suffering and find effective solutions to all the problems that you face. May you have the wisdom to discern and the courage to walk the path that reduces the greatest amount of suffering and generates the greatest amount of benefit for yourself and others. May all of your wholesome wishes and aspirations come true quickly and easily. And may this book serve as a guide to help you light your inner candle of goodness, tend to that flame as you reap the highest benefits of this practice, and inspire others around you to follow suit, thus creating a brighter world for all.

— Venerable Nick & Venerable Michael

ACCOUNTABILITY RESOURCES

Welcome to this final section! Here, you will find extra resources to help you succeed in starting and progressing down this path of creating a truly sustainable and transformative giving habit. Please scan the QR code below or enter the link into your browser to access and print these resources. We hope they enrich your spiritual journey. Enjoy!

https://nickkeomahavong.com/giving

HABIT TRACKERS

An invaluable tool that will help you stay accountable and track your progress is a habit tracker. The process of crossing off the days that you have completed your act of generosity is very satisfying—you get to see a physical representation of how far you have come and feel proud of yourself each day that you follow through on your commitment. Day by day, tick mark by tick mark, you build a stronger and stronger foundation. You feel more accomplished and motivated to continue. This process can be very fun and exciting, so enjoy!

The habit trackers that follow will give you a few ideas of different formats that you can utilize to help you track your progress. If you would like to download and print any of these habit trackers, then you can do so on our website.

1 MONTH HABIT TRACKER

SUN	MON	TUE	WED	THU	FRI	SAT

Insights from this month

7 WEEK HABIT TRACKER

Start date: _____

S	M	T	W	T	F	S

How do you feel after . . .

Week 1:   Week 4:   Week 7:

Week 2:   Week 5:

Week 3:   Week 6:

1 YEAR HABIT TRACKER 2024

January

S	M	T	W	T	F	S
	1	2	3	4	5	6
7	8	9	10	11	12	13
14	15	16	17	18	19	20
21	22	23	24	25	26	27
28	29	30	31			

February

S	M	T	W	T	F	S
				1	2	3
4	5	6	7	8	9	10
11	12	13	14	15	16	17
18	19	20	21	22	23	24
25	26	27	28	29		

March

S	M	T	W	T	F	S
					1	2
3	4	5	6	7	8	9
10	11	12	13	14	15	16
17	18	19	20	21	22	23
24	25	26	27	28	29	30
31						

April

S	M	T	W	T	F	S
	1	2	3	4	5	6
7	8	9	10	11	12	13
14	15	16	17	18	19	20
21	22	23	24	25	26	27
28	29	30				

May

S	M	T	W	T	F	S
			1	2	3	4
5	6	7	8	9	10	11
12	13	14	15	16	17	18
19	20	21	22	23	24	25
26	27	28	29	30	31	

June

S	M	T	W	T	F	S
						1
2	3	4	5	6	7	8
9	10	11	12	13	14	15
16	17	18	19	20	21	22
23	24	25	26	27	28	29
30						

July

S	M	T	W	T	F	S
	1	2	3	4	5	6
7	8	9	10	11	12	13
14	15	16	17	18	19	20
21	22	23	24	25	26	27
28	29	30	31			

August

S	M	T	W	T	F	S
				1	2	3
4	5	6	7	8	9	10
11	12	13	14	15	16	17
18	19	20	21	22	23	24
25	26	27	28	29	30	31

September

S	M	T	W	T	F	S
1	2	3	4	5	6	7
8	9	10	11	12	13	14
15	16	17	18	19	20	21
22	23	24	25	26	27	28
29	30					

October

S	M	T	W	T	F	S
		1	2	3	4	5
6	7	8	9	10	11	12
13	14	15	16	17	18	19
20	21	22	23	24	25	26
27	28	29	30	31		

November

S	M	T	W	T	F	S
					1	2
3	4	5	6	7	8	9
10	11	12	13	14	15	16
17	18	19	20	21	22	23
24	25	26	27	28	29	30

December

S	M	T	W	T	F	S
1	2	3	4	5	6	7
8	9	10	11	12	13	14
15	16	17	18	19	20	21
22	23	24	25	26	27	28
29	30	31				

REFLECT AND RECONNECT

Journaling and reflection are powerful tools to help clarify your pure intentions and give in the most healing way. Articulating the effects that this act will have or has had on you and others can help you more effortlessly and effectively reconnect with a bright, positive frame of mind before, during, and after the act.

Feel free to write down the specific act that you have accomplished (or one that you plan to do in the future) followed by the corresponding answers to the questions that lie below. Coming back to this section either before the act to prepare the mind to be in the brightest state possible or after the act to reflect and reconnect with the positive spiritual energy that the act generated can be equally beneficial.

Use the following writing prompts to guide your journaling on the following two pages.

- What are the potential positive effects this act will have on others?
- What are the positive effects it will have on you?
- How will it make you feel when you perform the act?

Flesh out all of these things so that you can brighten your mind before the act and prepare yourself for a fruitful act of generosity. This will be a good reference to come back to before, during, and after giving.

REFLECT AND RECONNECT

List your intentions and the positive effects of your acts

REFLECT & RECONNECT

Details of Your Act

I will perform the act of _____ at the location

of _____ at the time of _____

and will give the amount of _____

Write Down Any Intentions, Insights, and Impactful Moments

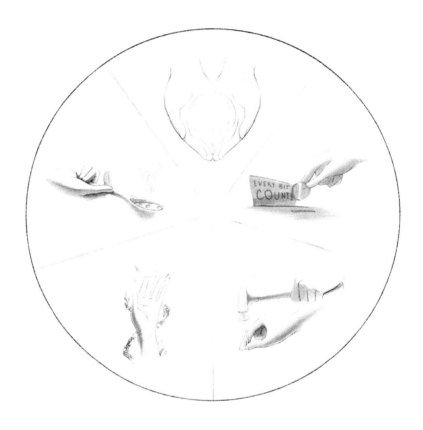

ENDING CONTENT

PAY IT FORWARD

https://nickkeomahavong.com/donate

Over the past roughly two years, Venerable Nick and Venerable Michael have given away over 12,000 free copies of their first two books to those who visited the meditation centers where they stay and have visited. This was all made possible by generous individuals who sponsored over twelve rounds of printing and shipping.

If you found this book or their previous books helpful and would like to be a part of sharing this wisdom and providing the gift of Dhamma to the world, you can make a donation to support printing and shipping costs for not only this book, but for all of the books Venerable Nick and Venerable Michael have written to date. For more details and to make a donation, please scan the QR code or visit the link provided above. Thank you for your generosity! We rejoice in your merit :)

ACKNOWLEDGMENTS

To our meditation masters, so much of the focus and intentions behind this book have stemmed from the wisdom that we have learned from you. We humbly hope that our efforts have preserved the integrity of your teachings and will serve to properly guide practitioners to practice giving in a way that you would hope for. We could never fully repay our debt of gratitude but hope that this book that makes your wisdom available to a Western audience makes you proud to have us as your sons in the Sangha. We are so grateful for your guidance and look forward to many more years of helping your vision of achieving world peace through inner peace become a reality. We rejoice in your immeasurable merit and share all of our merit with you.

To our teachers—Venerable Narongchai, Venerable Pawithai, our meditation teachers and tutors, and other spiritual mentors: We are eternally grateful for your support in creating a strong foundation for our monk life. Thank you for believing in us and giving us the space to grow and mature.

To Venerable Tim Dhiranando: Your artwork, as always, has brought our vision to life in a way that defies expectation. Co-creating the many spiritual resources we have produced thus far with you has been so fulfilling and enjoyable. We feel honored to give your work a platform to reach a broader audience and look forward to many more years of doing meritorious work together. We are so grateful for your support and friendship.

To Venerable Yao and Venerable Worawut: Thank you for always being so willing to help us research and have discussions to ensure that we are sharing the Dhamma accurately. We rejoice in your merit!

To Cleo: Your expertise, professionalism, and kindness played no small part in ensuring that our writing was well-polished and articulated eloquently and accurately. We look forward to collaborating on many more books into the future.

To the Singapore, Georgia, Azusa, and Pai meditation centers and the Pa Pae Meditation Retreat, thank you for giving us a space to grow, for your support in providing a place to distribute free copies of these books, and for helping to sponsor the printing costs. The gift of Dhamma is the highest gift, and you get a significant share in the merit of distributing this wisdom. We look forward to the next time we meet!

To each of our families, we would like to express our deepest gratitude. If it weren't for your love and sacrifice throughout our lives, we would certainly not be where we are today. So much of what we do is to repay the large debt of gratitude we have for all that you have given us. We would like to share all our merit from this lifetime with you.

To all of our teachers, friends, monk brothers, previous work colleagues, supervisors, and clients: Thank you for all the support, guidance, and encouragement along the way. You all played a significant part in our journey that led to the creation of this book, so we hope you enjoyed the read and can benefit from the content. Stay tuned for the next one!

ABOUT THE AUTHORS
Venerable Nick Santacitto

Ven. Nick, previously a practicing psychotherapist, has been ordained as a Theravada Buddhist monk in Thailand since 2018. His books capture his unique perspective by interweaving the tools of the mental health world and the wisdom from the monastery into simple and practical guides to healing. His YouTube channel also embodies a similar approach to sharing practical wisdom.

In addition to being a professional dancer, Ven. Nick acquired a diverse range of professional experience over the span of ten years in the mental health field before becoming a monk. This includes but is not limited to his roles as the lead clinician at a foster home for over one hundred kids ages twelve through eighteen; a program therapist at a drug treatment center in Malibu, California; a bereavement counselor at a hospice; and the founder and owner of his private practice, True Nature Counseling Center in San Diego, California.

However, at the pinnacle of his professional success, Ven. Nick left it all behind and became a monk in Thailand in order to become a more refined practitioner of the tools he was teaching. This is the journey he continues as he actualizes his highest mission of sharing this knowledge with others in order to help them discover their true nature and live congruently via their most authentic lives.

ABOUT THE AUTHORS
Venerable Michael Viradhammo

After discovering the healing power of Buddhism and meditation, Ven. Michael decided to abandon material pursuits and left his hometown of Atlanta, Georgia, to ordain as a Buddhist monk in Thailand, where he has been a monk since 2017. After ordaining, Ven. Michael spent much of his time teaching meditation and wisdom to travelers at the Pa Pae Meditation retreat in Chiang Mai as well as teaching and mentoring men who were becoming monks with the international ordination program.

He is also an avid writer pursuing his passion by cowriting books about practical wisdom to help readers overcome their suffering with Ven. Nick. Outside of sharing wisdom via their books, both monks also run events, create many helpful resources, and travel around the world on a shared mission to bridge mental health with spiritual health. Ven. Michael is deeply dedicated to continuously aligning his life with his true nature and helping others do the same.

CONNECT WITH
THE AUTHORS

 Visit a page that houses all of the links found below via the following link or QR code: https://bento.me/venerablenick

Access a growing catalogue of simple guided meditation audios led by the monks (Initial audios will be uploaded by April 2024): https://nickkeomahavong.com/meditation-audio

Learn the basics and practice at home with friends via these 1- and 3-day video-led meditation retreats guided by the monks: https://nickkeomahavong.com/retreats

Get a better feel for the broad range of topics, concepts, and stories that Venerable Nick has to share by visiting his YouTube channel: Nick Keomahavong.

Stay updated with any new resources, products, or other announcements by signing up for Venerable Nick's mailing list: tinyurl.com/nickkeomahavong